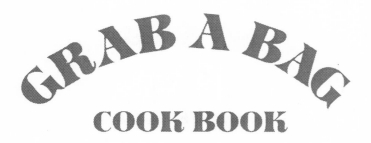

COOK BOOK

RECIPES THAT BEGIN IN A BAG WITH THE DRY INGREDIENTS
AND ARE COMPLETED LATER WITH THE LIQUID INGREDIENTS

GREAT FOR GIFTS, GUESTS AND GATHERINGS

FATHER & SON

PUBLISHING, INC.

4909 N. Monroe Street
Tallahassee, Florida 32303
http://www.fatherson.com

GRAB A BAG

RECIPES FOR QUICK MEALS, SNACKS, AND BEVERAGES

GRAB A BAG FROM THE PANTRY SHELF AND
COMPLETE IN A JIFFY

ASSEMBLE THE DRY INGREDIENTS

SEAL IN A PLASTIC BAG

COMPLETE LATER WITH THE LIQUID INGREDIENTS

GREAT FOR GIFTS, GUESTS
AND GATHERINGS

YOU HAVE BAG CONTROL
NO SUGAR...LESS SUGAR...SUGAR SUBSTITUTE
CAFFEINE...NO CAFFEINE
SALT...LESS SALT...NO SALT...SALT SUBSTITUTE
ELIMINATE A SPICE...ADD A SPICE...
SUBSTITUTE A SPICE OR HERB

YOU KNOW WHAT IS IN THE BAG

Dedicated
To
My
Husband
Bruno
To
My
Daughters
Angie, Beth, Cindy
To
My
Grandchildren
Sara, Morgan, Zachary, Sidney, Hannah
To
My
Son-in-law
Michael
And
To
My
Mother
Sara

Contents

ABOUT THE AUTHOR

Frances Barrineau is a native South Carolinian. She was educated in South Carolina but moved away after marriage. Her husband's career took her away from her hometown of Lancaster and she did not return to live until his retirement. They have returned to their hometown and built a home there.

The cookbook was started, put on the shelf, and started again many times. With encouragement from her family and friends the book was completed. She never attended any formal cooking schools but was fortunate to have a mother and grandmother who taught her all the basics.

"I never wanted to be gourmet cook," she says, "but I did want good food that could be prepared with little effort without buying prepackaged or frozen food. I like to know what is in the food I am eating and serving to my family and friends or giving as gifts."

The idea of the bags resulted from being away from her kitchen, trying to prepare a recipe and not having the necessary ingredients, especially the spices and herbs. These items can be expensive to buy for just one teaspoonful or one tablespoonful when you already have them in your kitchen. It is so much easier and less expensive just to prepare them at home and put in a plastic bag. It not only saves money but also time.

She loves to create and find better ways of doing things. She believes in recycling and also likes the challenge of making something from nothing or using an item in a different way.

She lives with her husband and three cats, none that was chosen except for the husband. Cats have a way of finding her house. She has three daughters and five grandchildren.

INTRODUCTION

I have developed the recipes in this book because I wanted to control the ingredients in the bag, and at the same time, I wanted a quick alternative to frozen meals.

Instead of cooking meals in advance and freezing, to use at a later date, I choose to prepare the bags in advance, buy the additional ingredients needed to complete and stock my pantry shelf rather than my freezer shelf. I find the food is fresher and easier to prepare. It also tastes better. The bags travel better than frozen foods, when preparing the recipes outside of your kitchen.

Since the bags and additional ingredients do not need refrigeration, it makes them perfect to take on camping trips, on vacation trips, for college dorms, parties, family gatherings, unexpected guests, and gifts. Husbands and older children love the bags when mom has to be away. They can cook and have good meals with the easy to follow instructions. There aren't a lot of pots and pans to wash either, since most of the recipes can be completed with just one utensil.

Always use resealable plastic bags for your bagged ingredients. They can be purchased in a paper goods store in all sizes. For my own pantry shelf and for my own individual use, I use the resealable plastic sandwich bags. They are cheaper and work quite well. Always label your bags so you will know which ingredients are inside. They can sometimes look alike. When I am giving the bag as a gift or when I am taking it with me, away from my kitchen, I always insert the plastic bag with the ingredients into a paper bag or a decorative bag and include the recipe for completing. If I am preparing the recipe in my own kitchen, I refer to my cookbook for the recipe to complete.

There is no need to include the recipe for the bag when giving as a gift, unless you wish or if the person who is receiving the bag has to limit sugar, salt, caffeine, etc. In this case you may wish to list the ingredients contained in the recipe for the bag.

Since the recipes for the bags contain no preservatives, there is a limit to the shelf life. The spices and herbs begin to lose their flavor and some of the ingredients will cake or harden. Plan to use in four to six weeks.

BAGS AND TAGS

A quick way to bag is to insert the plastic bag into a brown or white paper lunch bag. Write the recipe for completing directly on the bag. Fold over the top of the bag, punch two holes with a hole puncher, insert ribbon, twine, yarn, jute or a fabric strip and tie a bow. For your own personal use, you may simply wish to staple the bag.

Bags may also be made of fabric. Cut a piece of material 20" long and 8" wide. The short ends may be hemmed, pinked with pinking shears, or fringed. Fold evenly, short ends together with the right sides facing each other. Sew, using 5/8" seam allowances, on each side. Turn and press. After the ingredients are inserted, bunch up the top and tie with ribbon, jute, yarn, etc., about 2 to 3 inches from the top. For larger or smaller bags, adjust the length and width of the fabric.

Cookie and beverage bags are fun to make. Use heavy duty brown wrapping paper. Cut pieces 12" long and 5" wide. Fold to the inside a 1" hem on each short end, then fold in half, short ends meeting. Do not turn. Long edges may be pinked. Punch two holds on each side at the top. Cut 2 pieces of yarn or jute or twisted paper about 12" long. Insert one end of the yarn into a hole, front to inside. Tie a knot in the end, large enough so that it will not slip through the hole. Do the same for the other end. Repeat the process on the other side. Pull up the handles. On the outside write "HAVE A COOKIE AND A CUP OF TEA ON ME" TO _____ FROM _____. Insert an individual serving of spiced tea with the instructions to make and one of your special cookies sealed in plastic wrap. Hang on the doorknob of an office friend or special neighbor.

Stencil bags for holidays or special occasions, such as " MERRY CHRISTMAS" or "HAPPY BIRTHDAY," etc.

Fold white index cards, either top to bottom or side to side, for great inexpensive bag holders. On the front, draw or write a message. On one side of an inside flap, write a recipe for completing and on the other side tape or staple the bag of dry ingredients. Tie with appropriate ribbon.

Fold a brown piece of paper, envelope style. Staple the top, inserting a short piece of string in the staple. On the other end,

attach a small square of white heavy duty paper about 1" by 1."
Write instructions for preparing on the square and tuck a small
bag of spiced tea into the folded brown paper. Make to resemble
a tea bag. Stick several into a mug for a nice gift or fill a small
basket with tea bags and give to a friend for tea anytime.
Enclose basket with cellophane and tie with a silver ribbon or
cord.

Cellophane bags may also be purchased to use when giving
your recipe bags. You can find them for all occasions and holidays. Some of the Christmas cellophane bags look especially
nice tied with gold or silver ribbons or cords.

Tags can be made from almost anything, as can recipe cards.
Recycle Christmas cards, thank you cards, birthday cards, etc.
for your projects. Keep a box for your collections.

Save bags, paper, ribbon, lace, string, yarn, fabric scraps, etc.
Keep only the front of the cards. Discard the rest. Write the
recipe for completing on the back. Punch two holes at the top
and insert the ribbon before you tie it to the bag. Let the pic-
ture face out and the recipe towards the bag. Be sure to note
on the front that the recipe can be found on the back.

A country card looks best with brown paper or burlap bags
and used for jambalaya or bean soup. A snow scene on a white
bag is good for coffee, apple grog or winter warmer.

A Christmas card works well for holiday pancakes or
Christmastide tea. Get the idea? Leftover gift tags work well
too, for short recipes and small bags.

When making fabric bags, use a material that compliments
the recipe. For example, a cow print for hot chocolate, an apple
print for hot apple grog or caramel apples. An apple print is a
good choice for a teacher's gift too. Tie on a small slate as a
bag ornament. Write on the slate with white chalk or white
acrylic paint. On the slate you may write TO _____ FROM
_____ or ABC or 123 or $1 + 1 = 2$. You may even draw a small
apple in one corner or use an apple sticker. The slate could later
be used as a Christmas ornament or peg decoration.

Remember! Never throw anything away until you have recycled
it, if possible. Recycle grocery bags made of heavy brown paper.
Cut away the advertising, iron out the wrinkles with a warm iron
and keep for later use.

Another idea is to make a spaghetti basket. Include the spice bag, spaghetti noodles and all the other needed ingredients, except the meat. You could also tuck in tongs, a spaghetti server or noodle measurer. Bunch cellophane around the basket and tie with a ribbon. Baskets filled with an assortment of beverages or dips also make nice holiday gifts.

Plastic freezer bags with the twist tabs make good containers for beverage mixes. Tie with a narrow ribbon for color. You may also add a small bag of marshmallows or tie on cinnamon sticks, depending on the beverage given.

Include a muffin tin or aluminum foil muffin pan with a muffin mix. Wrap in cellophane or with a pretty kitchen towel or apron. You may also include muffin tin liners or several hot pads. This makes a nice gift for a bridal shower. Another bridal gift would be a large cookie sheet with the cookie mix or a big cookie jar with the cookie mix.

Give a new neighbor a quick soup mix with all the additional ingredients needed to complete. Include paper soup bowls, spoons, soup crackers and napkins that say "Welcome." They will be happy that they moved into your neighborhood.

When a friend comes home from the hospital with a new baby, bag a complete meal. You may choose "Beef Stew in a Wink" or "Pesto and Pasta", with "Quick Peach Cobbler" as dessert. Include a loaf of French bread and a package of napkins with a baby motif and maybe a baby toy. Even if the new dad doesn't cook, he can prepare this meal.

Be sure to include the recipes for completing.

A new bride may like a casserole recipe tucked into a useful oven proof dish in just the right size to accommodate the recipe. Why not include the "GRAB A BAG" cookbook too?

Need a graduation gift for a college bound friend? Purchase a book bag and stuff with recipe bags that can be completed in the dorm room. Good choices would be beverages, snacks, and soups.

MAKE YOUR OWN RECIPE CARDS

Use 3" x 5" index cards.
Fold the card in half, short sides together.
Punch a hole in the upper left corner with a hole puncher.
Pink the bottom on the front side or leave it plain.
Trace, cut out and color selected patterns using another index card.
Glue pattern to the top of the folded index card.
Write the name of the recipe on the front.
Write the recipe for completing on the inside.
Loop a piece of ribbon or tie of choice through the hole and attach to the bag containing the bagged ingredients.
(For full sized patterns and instructions, see pages 198-200.)

GIFT GIVING IDEAS
There is no limit to the ideas for gift giving!

Use a pretty dishtowel or dishcloth. Tuck the bagged ingredients inside the towel or cloth. Stick in a wooden spoon, tongs, ladle, etc. Tie it all up with ribbon, jute, or yarn.

Insert a bag of ingredients into a pretty oven mitt. Make a pretty bag ornament and tie on. Let the ornament fit the occasion. An idea would be to paint a wooden heart with an off white paint. Write on the heart a message such as "KISS THE COOK." You may also wish to stencil a country house under the message for a finished look.

Tuck a single serving of tea or cocoa into a pretty mug or paper hot cup. Look for mugs at tag sales or clearance sales. Why not give everyone at the office a paper hot cup, serving of tea, and a plastic or wooden spoon or stick for stirring? Cut a square of cellophane and bunch around the cup. Tie with a pretty ribbon and leave on the desk.

This is guaranteed to brighten the day!

Cut two pieces of heavy brown paper into 6" x 6" squares. Hold the two pieces together and punch holes at each corner through both pieces. Then, punch 6 holes between the corner holes, also, through both pieces, until you have holes on all four sides. Write the recipe for completing on one side. Insert the bagged ingredients. Lace yarn or ribbon around the entire outside edge. Leave enough yarn or ribbon at each end to tie a pretty bow. This idea works well for a beverage or a dip.

Stick a bag of "Winter Warmer" (potato soup) and a bag of soup crackers into a pretty soup bowl or large mug. Give as a gift or take to a sick friend or neighbor on a cold dreary day.

For Christmas, I usually give my neighbors baskets filled with some of my recipe bags. I usually include a soup, beverage, dip, jambalaya or rice. You could also make baskets for other occasions. For New Years, let your basket include Black-eyed Rice and Cornbread muffins. Tuck in New Years' hats or horns and napkins for a colorful touch.

Appetizers and Snacks

APPETIZERS

Salmon Spread

Recipe for the bag:

3	tablespoons chopped dried green onions or chives
1	tablespoon dried parsley flakes
1	tablespoon cilantro leaves
½	teaspoon cayenne pepper
½	teaspoon paprika

Combine all the ingredients and store in a plastic bag.

Recipe for completing:

1	(8oz.) package of lite cream cheese, softened
1	teaspoon lime juice
1	(6⅛ oz.) can chunk style salmon, drained and flaked contents of the bag

Stir the cream cheese and the lime juice until smooth. Beat until fluffy. Add the contents of the bag. Stir in the salmon. Cover and refrigerate. Serve with crackers or melba rounds. (10 to 12 servings)

DILLY DIP FOR FRESH VEGETABLES

Recipe for the bag:

1	tablespoon dried parsley flakes
1	tablespoon dried chopped onions
½	tablespoon dried dill weed
¼	teaspoon celery salt
⅛	teaspoon garlic powder
⅛	teaspoon mustard powder

Mix all the ingredients and store in a small plastic bag.

Recipe for completing:

1 cup sour cream
1 cup mayonnaise
Contents of the bag

Mix together the sour cream and the mayonnaise. Stir in the contents of the bag. If too thick, stir in a little milk, until the right consistancy is achieved. Serve with assorted fresh vegetables, such as broccoli, cauliflower, carrot sticks, celery sticks, green onions, sliced cucumbers, etc.

For a fat-free dip, use a no fat mayonnaise and a fat-free sour cream alternative. If too thick, stir in a little fat-free milk until the right consistency is achieved.

SOUTH OF THE BORDER DIP

Recipe for the bag:

3 tablespoons onion powder
3 tablespoons chili powder
3 tablespoons cornstarch
1 tablespoon dried oregano
2 teaspoons ground cumin
1 teaspoon dried cilantro leaves
1 teaspoon garlic powder
1 teaspoon paprika
3 packages low sodium beef flavored bouillon granules
   (about 1 ½ tablespoons)
1/8 teaspoon salt
1/8 teaspoon white pepper
1/8 teaspoon red pepper or cayenne pepper

Mix all the ingredients and store in a plastic bag. (may store in individual amounts of 3 tablespoons each.)

Recipe for completing:

1 cup mayonnaise
1 cup sour cream
1 small grated onion
1 (4 oz.) can chopped black olives, drained
1 (4 oz.) can chopped mild green chili peppers, drained
3 tablespoons seasoning mix from the bag

Mix the sour cream and the mayonnaise. Stir in the grated onion, olives, chili peppers, and 3 tablespoons seasoning mix. Serve with taco chips. (yield about 2 cups)

HOT HOLIDAY SPREAD

Recipe for the bag:

1   teaspoon dried cilantro leaves, crushed
½   teaspoon chili powder
½   teaspoon paprika
⅛   teaspoon cumin
⅛   teaspoon mustard powder

Mix all the ingredients and store in a plastic bag.

Recipe for completing:

8   oz. cream cheese, softened
4   tablespoons hot pepper jelly
Contents of the bag

Mix the cream cheese and the jelly. Stir in the contents of the bag. Serve with wheat or vegetable crackers. (yield about 1 cup)

SPICY CHICKEN BITES

Recipe for the bag:

½   cup Italian bread crumbs
1   package dried onion soup mix
1   (1.25 oz.) package of taco seasoning mix or 3
      tablespoons taco seasoning mix found in the ET
      CETERA section of this book

Mix all the ingredients and store in a plastic bag.

Recipe for completing:

2 Lbs. chicken breast fillets (cut into 1" bite size pieces)
¼ cup melted margarine
Contents of the bag

Empty the contents of the bag into a medium sized brown paper bag. Drop the chicken pieces, a few at the time, into the bag and shake to coat. Repeat the process until all the pieces are coated. Preheat the oven to 350 degrees. Melt the margarine in an oven proof dish. Arrange the coated chicken on top of the margarine in a single layer. Bake for about 30 minutes, turning once. This is a good party food. Prepare ahead of time and stick in the oven ½ hour before serving time. Serve with honey mustard dressing. Yields 10 to 12 servings.

HERBED BAGEL ROUNDS

Recipe for the bag:

1	teaspoon garlic powder
1	teaspoon parsley flakes, crushed
1	teaspoon ground oregano
1	teaspoon basil leaves, crushed
1	teaspoon onion powder
1/2	teaspoon paprika

Mix all the ingredients and store in a plastic bag.

Recipe for completing:

6	plain or onion bagels, uncut type
1	stick margarine or butter, melted
	Contents of the bag

Slice the bagels into thin rounds. Place in a large bowl. Mix the contents of the bag with the melted margarine or butter. Pour over the bagel rounds, tossing well to coat. Spread on cookie sheets or pieces of heavy duty aluminum foil that have been doubled. Cook in a preheated oven at 300 degrees for 30 to 45 minutes, stirring occasionally, or until crisp. Store in an airtight container. (Recipe may be haved, 3 bagels, $1/2$ margarine or butter and $1/2$ the contents of the bag)

STRAWBERRIES AND CREAM DIP

Recipe for the bag:

¼ cup powdered sugar
1   (3oz.) package strawberry-banana gelatin
1   teaspoon vanilla powder

Mix all the ingredients and store in a plastic bag.

Recipe for completing:

1   (8 oz.) package cream cheese, softened
3   tablespoons strawberry preserves
Orange juice
Contents of the bag

Stir the contents of the bag into the softened cream cheese. Add the strawberry preserves and enough orange juice for a good consistency, for either a dip or a spread. Serve as a dip for fresh orange slices, banana chunks, or fresh strawberries or use as a spread for nut bread, sugar cookies, or vanilla wafers. (yield about 1 cup)

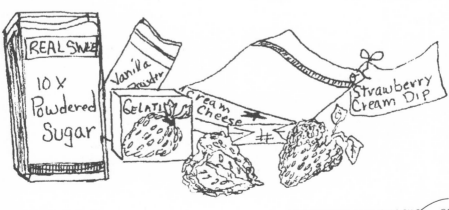

CAJUN RAGE

Recipe for the bag:

1	teaspoon paprika
1	teaspoon garlic powder
1	teaspoon ground thyme
1	teaspoon ground oregano
1	teaspoon cumin
1	teaspoon chili powder

Mix all the ingredients and store in a plastic bag.

Recipe for completing:

1	(16 oz.) bag of tortilla chips
½	cup grated Parmesan cheese
¼	cup vegetable oil
	Contents of the bag

Mix the contents of the bag with the oil. Empty the chips into a large container and pour the oil mixture over the chips. Stir until the chips are coated. Put the coated chips into a roasting pan and sprinkle the cheese over the chips. Stir again. Bake in a preheated 200 degree oven for about 30 minutes stirring every 10 minutes. Empty into a large brown paper bag. Shake well and let sit in the bag until ready to serve. This absorbs some of the oil.

ZUCCHINI BITES

Recipe for the bag:

1   cup biscuit mix (may use the reduced-fat type)
½   cup grated Parmesan cheese
2   tablespoons chopped dried onions
1   teaspoon oregano leaves
1   teaspoon garlic powder
⅛   teaspoon white pepper
⅛   teaspoon salt (optional)

Mix all the ingredients and store in a plastic bag.

Recipe for completing:

3   cups unpeeled grated zucchini squash
4   eggs, beaten
½   cup olive oil
Contents of the bag

Combine the eggs and the oil. Stir in the contents of the bag. Fold in the grated zucchini. Bake in a greased 13" x 9" x 2" pan or baking dish for 30 minutes in a 350 degree preheated oven. Cut into bite size squares or fingers. Serve hot. (yield depends on the size of the squares or fingers)

YUMMY SWEET SNAX

Recipe for the bag:

1 (16 oz.) package candy coated chocolate pieces
1 (16 oz.) box raisins
1 (16 oz.) can mixed nuts
1 (12 oz.) package vanilla pieces or chips
1 (6 oz.) package butterscotch pieces
1 (6 oz.) package semisweet chocolate pieces or chips
1 (6 oz.) package peanut butter pieces
1 cup dried banana slices (optional)

Mix all the ingredients in a large container. Divide into equal portions and seal in individual plastic bags. (yield depends on the size of the portions)

Recipe for completing:

1 bag of mix.
The only recipe needed here is a card that reads " OPEN-REACH IN-ENJOY!!!" Makes a great Valentine gift for your sweethearts.

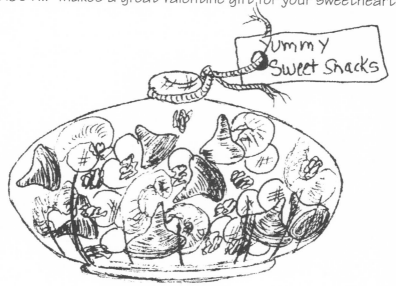

KIDS BEAR SNACKS

Recipe for the bag:

1   cup chocolate bear cookies
1   cup vanilla bear cookies
1   cup cinnamon bear cookies
1   cup apple-cinnamon round oat cereal
1   cup raisins
1   cup small jelly beans or gummi bears
1   cup candy coated chocolate pieces or chocolate
       coated peanut butter pieces

Mix all the ingredients in a large bowl. Store in a large resealable plastic bag.

Recipe for completing:

Take a few servings at the time from the bag when ready to eat or take individual servings and seal in small bags. This makes an excellent party favor or school treat. Grown-ups like it, too!! (yield depends on the size of the servings)

SPICY STICKS N' NUTS

Recipe for the bag:

2   (3 oz.) cans French fried onion rings
1   (7 oz.) can potato sticks
1   (3 oz.) can chow mein noodles
2   cups pretzel sticks
2   cups dry roasted peanuts
3   tablespoons taco seasoning mix found in the ET
     CETERA section of this cookbook or you may use 1 (1
     ¼ oz.) packet of premixed taco seasoning.

Combine all the ingredients and store in a large plastic bag.
Shake to mix.

Recipe for completing:

1   stick butter or margarine
     Contents of the bag

Melt the margarine or butter in a large roasting pan or other
large pan with sides. Stir in the contents of the bag, coating
well. Bake at 250 degrees for 1 hour, stirring mix every 15 minutes. Cut open a large brown paper bag. Empty the mix onto the
bag. Spread and cool. Store in 2 resealable quart bags. Keep one
for yourself and give the other to a friend to enjoy. (yield 2
quarts)

MARINATED PIMIENTO OLIVES

Recipe for the bag:

1   tablespoon dried chives
2   teaspoons minced dry garlic
1   teaspoon dried tarragon
½   teaspoon whole black peppercorns

Mix all the ingredients and store in a plastic bag.

Recipe for completing:

1   (8 oz.) jar green olives, stuffed
¼   cup white wine vinegar
¼   cup olive oil
Contents of the bag

Place the drained olives in a glass container with a lid. Combine the oil and vinegar. Stir in the contents of the bag. Pour over the olives. Secure the lid and shake vigorously so that the olives are well coated. Marinate at room temperature for 2 days. Shake the jar daily. Drain before serving. Yields 1 cup of olives. Recipe can be doubled.

CHILI CHEDDAR CHEESE BALL

Recipe for the bag:

¼ cup chopped pecans
1 teaspoon chili powder
1 teaspoon paprika
½ teaspoon garlic powder
¼ teaspoon Beau Monde seasoning

Mix all the ingredients and store in a plastic bag.

Recipe for completing:

2 cups grated cheddar cheese
1 (3 oz.) package cream cheese, softened
1 tablespoon lemon juice
Contents of the bag

Mix the cream cheese with the lemon juice. Combine with the cheddar cheese. (Use your hands) Shape into 1 large or 2 small balls. Roll the ball in the contents of the bag until completely covered. Wrap in plastic wrap. Store in the refrigerator. This freezes well for several weeks. Serve at room temperature with assorted crackers.

PORCUPINE APPETIZERS

Recipe for the bag:

½   cup minute rice
1   tablespoon minced dry onion
¼   teaspoon salt
¼   teaspoon dried basil
¼   teaspoon dried oregano
¼   teaspoon curry powder
¼   teaspoon mustard powder

Combine all the ingredients and store in a plastic bag.

Recipe for completing:

1   lb. ground beef
1   (8 oz.) can tomato sauce
½   cup water
2   tablespoons tomato catsup
1   tablespoon Worcestershire sauce
Contents of the bag

Combine the catsup, Worcestershire sauce, and the contents of the bag with the ground beef. Mix with your hands. Shape into tablespoon size balls. Use a scoop, if you have one. If not, measure out tablespoon portions and then roll into balls. Place balls into a shallow oven proof dish. I use a 10" glass pie plate. Combine the tomato sauce and the water. Pour over the meat balls. Cover and bake in a 350 degree oven for 1 hour, turning several times. Uncover and bake another 20 to 30 minutes. Serve as an appetizer using toothpicks or wooden skewers. (Makes 19 meat balls)

CUCUMBER AND ONION DIP

Recipe for the bag:

2   teaspoons garlic powder
½   teaspoon dried dill weed
½   teaspoon dried parsley flakes
½   teaspoon celery salt
¼   teaspoon ground white pepper

Combine all the ingredients and store in a resealable plastic bag.

Recipe for completing:

1   (8 oz.) package cream cheese, softened
1   medium cucumber, unpeeled
1   medium sweet onion, peeled
1   tablespoon mayonaise
1   tablespoon milk
Contents of the bag

Grate the cucumber and the onion. Set aside. Combine the cream cheese, mayonaise, milk and the contents of the bag. Drain off any water from the cucumber and onion andadd the vegetables to the cream cheese mixture. Stir well to blend. Serve with ruffled potato chips. (Makes 2 cups)

Beverages

BEVERAGES

CHRISTMASTIDE TEA

Recipe for the bag:

1   (15 oz.) jar orange breakfast crystals or 2 to 2½
cups crystals
1   (4 oz.) jar instant orange spice herbal sugar free,
decaffeinated tea or 3 cups
1   (3 oz.) package pineapple-orange gelatin
1   (0.46 oz.) package presweetened lemonade mix
3   teaspoons ground cinnamon
1   teaspoon ground cloves

Mix all the ingredients and divide into small bags for individual servings and larger bags for more than one serving. (Makes about 4 (1 cup) packages or 70 (1 tablespoon) single serving packs.

Recipe for completing:

Add 1 tablespoon of mix to 8 oz. boiling water. Stir well. This is for the larger bags.
Add 1 packet to 8 oz. boiling water. Stir well. This is for individual servings.

LOW-CAL-DECAF HOT SPICED TEA

Recipe for the bag:

1   cup decaffeinated instant tea
1   (0.15 oz.) package unsweetened orange drink mix
1   (0.15 oz.) package unsweetened lemonade drink mix
1   (0.3 oz.) package sugar free Hawaiian pineapple gelatin
12   packages sugar substitute
1   teaspoon ground cloves
1   teaspoon ground cinnamon
1   teaspoon ground allspice
¼   teaspoon dried orange peel
¼   teaspoon dried lemon peel

Combine all the ingredients and store in large or small bags, according to the size of the servings. (Makes 25 servings of 1 heaping teaspoon.)

Recipe for completing:

Stir 1 heaping teaspoon of mix into 8 oz. boiling water. Stir well. If using single serving packs, recipe should read: Stir 1 packet of mix into 8 oz. boiling water. Stir well.

PINEAPPLE-ORANGE TEA

Recipe for the bag:

1	cup instant tea (regular or decaffeinated)
1	cup white granulated sugar
1	(3 oz.) package pineapple-orange gelatin

Mix all the ingredients. Blend well. Store in a resealable plastic bag.

Recipe for completing:

Combine 2 teaspoons of mix with 8 oz. boiling water. Stir well. (Yield about 48 servings)

CROCK-POT COCOA

Recipe for the bag:

3½ cups non-fat dry milk
½ cup white granulated sugar
½ cup unsweetened cocoa powder
1 teaspoon vanilla powder
1 teaspoon ground cinnamon

Mix all the ingredients and store in a plastic bag.

Recipe for completing:

4 cups water
2 cups milk
Contents of the bag
Miniature marshmallows

Empty the contents of the bag into a crock-pot. Add the water and the milk. Stir until well blended. Cook on low for 3 to 4 hours or on high for 1 to 1½ hours. When ready to serve, top with the miniature marshmallows. (12 servings)

BASIC INSTANT COCOA

Recipe for the bag:

2   cups dry non-fat milk
¼   cup cocoa
12   packets sugar substitute or 1 cup powdered sugar
     (depending on diet)
1   tablespoon vanilla powder

Mix all the ingredients and seal in large or small bags depending on the size of the servings.

Recipe for completing:

Mix 2 level tablespoons of mix with 8 oz. of boiling water. Stir well. Top with whipped topping or marshmallows. (18 to 20 servings)

HOT COCOA (NUT) MIX

Recipe for the bag:

3   cups dry non-fat milk
1   cup non-dairy creamer
1   cup powdered sugar
½   cup cocoa
1   tablespoon vanilla powder
1   (3.4 oz.) package instant coconut pudding and pie
     mix

Mix all the ingredients well. Divide into small bags for individual servings or larger bags for more than one serving.

Recipe for completing:

Add 3 tablespoons mix to 8 oz. of boiling water. Stir until well blended. Top with miniature marshmallows or whipped topping, if desired.
(About 30 servings)

HAPPY HALLOWEEN PUNCH

Recipe for the bag:

1   cup orange pineapple breakfast drink
½   cup granulated white sugar
1   (0.32 oz.) package unsweetened lemonade flavored
      drink mix

Combine all the ingredients and store in a plastic bag.

Recipe for completing:

1   cup water
2   (1 Liter) bottles of sparkling grape flavored water
Contents of the bag

Dissolve the contents of the bag in the cup of water. When ready to serve combine with the two bottles of flavored water. Serve over crushed ice. This is great for Halloween gatherings. (Makes 10 cups)

CINNAMON COFFEE

Recipe for the bag:

½ cup instant coffee granules (regular or decaffeinated)
½ cup non-fat dry milk
1   teaspoon cinnamon
1   teaspoon vanilla powder

Mix the ingredients and seal in a large plastic bag or several small bags, depending in the size of the servings.

Recipe for completing:

Add 1 tablespoon of mix to 6 oz. boiling water. Stir well. Sweeten to taste, using sugar or artificial sweetener. (About 16 servings)

SPICED COFFEE

Recipe for the bag:

1   (2 oz.) jar instant coffee granules
1   teaspoon ground cinnamon
1   teaspoon ground allspice
1   teaspoon pumpkin pie spice
1   teaspoon vanilla powder

Combine all the ingredients and seal in large or small plastic bags, depending on the size of the servings.

Recipe for completing:

Add 1 teaspoon coffee mix to 8 oz. of boiling water. Add sugar and cream to taste. (52 servings)

SPICED COFFEE CREAMER

Recipe for the bag:

1   cup non-dairy creamer
1   teaspoon vanilla powder
1   teaspoon ground cinnamon
1   teaspoon ground allspice

Mix the ingredients and seal in large or small plastic bags depending on the size of the servings.

Recipe for completing:

Add 1 teaspoon of creamer to 8 oz. of steaming hot coffee. Sweeten to taste. (51 servings)

HOT SPICED MOCHA MIX

Recipe for the bag:

1   cup non-fat dry milk
1   cup non-dairy coffee creamer
½   cup cocoa
½   cup instant coffee granules (may use
     decaffeinated)
1   tablespoon ground cinnamon

Mix all the ingredients and seal in a large or small bag depending on the size of the servings.

Recipe for completing:

Mix 2 tablespoons mocha mix with 8 oz. of boiling water. Stir well to blend. Sweeten according to taste. (Makes about 24 servings)

JACK FROSTY

Recipe for the bag:

2   tablespoons non-fat dry milk
1   tablespoon orange-pineapple breakfast drink
1   tablespoon granulated white sugar
¼   teaspoon vanilla powder

Combine all the ingredients and store in a plastic bag.

Recipe for completing:

¾   cup water
4 or 5 ice cubes
Contents of the bag

Empty the contents of the bag into a blender. Add the water and the ice cubes. Blend on high until the ice is crushed and mixture begins to thicken. The more ice cubes that are added, the thicker the mixture.   (1 serving)

PUNCH FOR A CROWD

Recipe for the bag:

1   (3 oz.) package lemon gelatin
1   (3 oz.) package lime gelatin
1   (3 oz.) package apricot gelatin
1   (3 oz.) package pineapple-orange gelatin
2   tubs instant tea with lemon

Combine all the ingredients and divide into 2 equal portions. Seal in plastic bags.

Recipe for completing:

1   (67.6 oz.) bottle cherry or cranberry ginger ale, chilled
4   cups hot water
4   cups cold water
    Contents of 1 bag

Dissolve the contents of 1 bag in the hot water. Add the cold water. Stir well and chill. When ready to serve, add the ginger ale. To double the recipe, use both bags of mix and double the water and ginger ale. (Makes 2 gallons when doubled)

HOT APPLE GROG

Recipe for the bag:

1	(3 oz.) package orange-pineapple gelatin
1	(.031 oz.) package unsweetened lemonade soft drink mix
1	cup granulated brown sugar
1	cup granulated white sugar
1	teaspoon ground cinnamon
½	teaspoon each ground nutmeg, cloves, ginger, allspice, and mace

Mix all the ingredients well. Divide into small bags for individual servings or larger bags for more than one serving. (Makes about 27 servings)

Recipe for completing:

Add 1 tablespoon of mix to 8 oz. of very hot apple juice. Stir well to blend.

CIDER SACHETS

Recipe for the bag:

2 cinnamon sticks (broken into small pieces)
1 tablespoon whole allspice
1 tablespoon whole cloves
1 tablespoon dried orange peel (broken into small pieces)*

Make a small bag from cheesecloth or cut a piece of cheese-cloth, doubled, into a 6" x 6" square. Put the spices in the middle. Draw the corners together and hold tightly. Tie a cotton string around the middle to secure. Tie onto the outside a stick of cinnamon for an added touch, if desired.

Recipe for completing:

2 quarts apple cider
1 cider sachet

Combine the cider and the sachet in a large pot. Be sure to remove the instruction tag. Simmer for 15 minutes. For 1 gallon of cider use 2 sachets. Simmer longer than 15 minutes if you desire a stronger spice flavor.

*Make your own dried orange peel. Peel a large orange. Remove as much of the white membrane as you can. Place the pieces on a cookie sheet and put into an oven set at 200 degrees. Heat for 30 minutes. Turn and heat for another 30 minutes. Remove from the oven. Cool and break into small pieces. One large orange will make about 2 tablespoons of peel.

Breads and Muffins

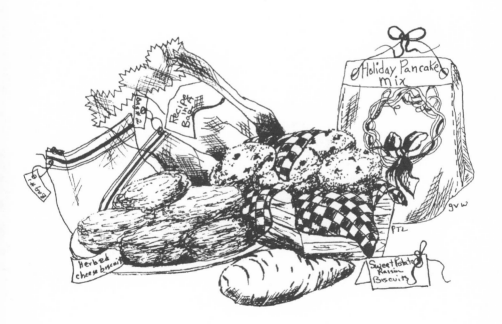

BREADS AND MUFFINS

SPICED OATMEAL MUFFINS

Recipe for the bag:

Bag # 1

1   cup quick cooking oats
1   cup granulated brown sugar
4   tablespoons dry cultured buttermilk

Bag # 2

1¾ cups self-rising flour
1   (1½ oz.) package snack size raisins
1   teaspoon ground cinnamon
1   teaspoon ground allspice
½   teaspoon dried orange peel
½   teaspoon dried lemon peel

Mix all the ingredients and store in separate bags. Label as bag
1 and bag # 2.

Recipe for completing:

1   cup water
1   egg, beaten
½   cup vegetable oil
1   (4 oz.) snack tub of applesauce
Contents of both bags

Mix the water with the beaten egg. Stir in the contents of bag
1. Let mixture sit for one hour. Add the contents of bag # 2,
the oil, and the applesauce. Pour into greased or paper lined
muffin tins. Fill ¾ full. Bake at 400 degrees for about 20
minutes. (Makes 18 muffins)

GRAHAM CRACKER MINI MUFFINS

Recipe for the bag:

1½ cups pecan pieces
1½ cups raisins
1   cup graham cracker crumbs
1   cup granulated brown sugar
1   teaspoon baking powder
1   teaspoon apple pie spice

Mix all the ingredients and store in a plastic bag.

Recipe for completing:

3   eggs, beaten
Contents of the bag

Add the contents of the bag to the beaten eggs. Stir until well blended. Grease mini muffin tins or line with paper liners. Fill muffin tins with 1 tablespoon of mix. Bake at 350 degrees for 15 to 20 minutes. (Makes about 2 dozen mini muffins)

HOLIDAY PANCAKE MIX

Recipe for the bag:

1	cup quick cooking oats
1	cup biscuit mix
¼	cup non-fat dry milk
¼	cup raisins
¼	cup dried mixed fruit (cut into pieces about the size of the raisins)
1	teaspoon ground cinnamon

Mix all the ingredients and store in a plastic bag.

Recipe for completing:

½	stick butter or margarine, melted
1	egg, beaten
1	cup water or ½ cup water and ½ cup milk
	Contents of the bag

Mix the melted butter or margarine and the beaten egg. Alternately add the contents of the bag and the water or the milk and water to the egg mixture. Drop by heaping tablespoons onto a greased hot griddle or skillet. Cook 2 or 3 minutes, turn, and continue cooking until lightly browned. Serve with melted butter or margarine and maple syrup.
(Makes about 3 dozen small pancakes)

BAG YOUR OWN CORN MUFFIN MIX

Recipe for the bag:

2/3 cup biscuit mix
1/3 cup corn meal
2   tablespoons non-fat dry milk
2   teaspoons granulated white sugar

Combine all the ingredients and store in a plastic bag.

Recipe for completing:

1/2 cup milk
1   egg, beaten
Contents of the bag

Combine the egg and the milk. Add the contents of the bag, a little at the time. Stir until smooth. Fill greased muffin tins 3/4 full. Bake at 450 degrees for 20 minutes. (Makes 6 muffins)

HERBED CHEESE BISCUITS

Recipe for the bag:

2	cups biscuit mix
1/2	teaspoon garlic powder
1/2	teaspoon dried Italian seasoning
1/2	teaspoon paprika
1/8	teaspoon ground red pepper

Combine all the ingredients and store in a plastic bag.

Recipe for completing:

1	cup grated cheddar cheese
1/2	cup cold water
1/2	stick butter or margarine, melted
	Contents of the bag

Combine the contents of the bag with the water. Stir in the cheese and the melted margarine or butter. Drop in heaping tablespoon portions onto a greased baking sheet. Bake at 450 degrees for 10 to 12 minutes. (Makes about 16 biscuits)

SWEET POTATO-RAISIN DROP BISCUITS

Recipe for the bag:

2   cups biscuit mix (may use the reduced-fat variety)
2   tablespoons granulated white sugar
1   teaspoon ground cinnamon
½   teaspoon ground nutmeg
⅛   teaspoon ground mace
2   (1½ oz.) boxes of raisins or ¾ cup

Combine all the ingredients and store in a plastic bag.

Recipe for completing:

1   (15 oz.) can sweet potatoes, drained (may use fresh
     cooked sweet potatoes to equal 1 cup mashed
     potatoes)
½   cup milk
Contents of the bag

Gradually add the milk to the mashed sweet potatoes. Stir in
½ the contents of the bag and mix well. Stir in the remainder of
the contents of the bag and continue to mix until you have good
stiff dough. Drop by heaping tablespoons onto a greased cookie
sheet. Bake at 450 degrees for about 20 minutes. Serve with
butter and honey.
(Makes about 1 dozen biscuits)

APPLESAUCE RAISIN MUFFINS

Recipe for the bag:

2	cups self-rising flour
1	cup raisins
½	cup granulated white sugar
½	cup granulated brown sugar
1	teaspoon ground cinnamon
1	teaspoon ground allspice
1	teaspoon vanilla powder
½	teaspoon ground cloves

Combine all the ingredients and store in a plastic bag.

Recipe for completing:

1	stick butter or margarine, melted
1	egg, beaten
1	cup applesauce
	Contents of the bag

Stir together the melted margarine or butter, egg, and the applesauce. Gradually add the contents of the bag. Fill paper lined muffin tins about ⅔ full. Bake at 350 degrees for 15 to 20 minutes or until browned. (Makes about 15 medium muffins)

ZUCCHINI NUT BREAD

Recipe for the bag:

1½ cups all purpose flour
1   cup granulated white sugar
½   cup raisins
½   cup chopped pecans
1   teaspoon vanilla powder
1   teaspoon ground cinnamon
½   teaspoon salt
½   teaspoon baking powder
½   teaspoon baking soda

Combine all the ingredients and store in a plastic bag.

Recipe for completing:

2   eggs, beaten
1   cup zucchini squash, peeled and grated
½   cup vegetable oil
¼   cup sour cream
Contents of the bag

Grease and flour a 9" x 5" loaf pan. Combine all the ingredients and mix until just moistened well. Do not over mix. Pour into the loaf pan. Bake at 350 degrees for 1 hour and 15 minutes. Let cool before removing from pan. When cooled, remove from pan. Slice and serve. (Makes 8 to 10 servings)

Soups and Stews

SOUPS

BEAN AND PASTA SOUP
Recipe for the bag:
Bag # 1

1   cup instant potato flakes
½   cup dried vegetable flakes
½   cup dried chopped onions
½   cup dried celery flakes
½   cup beef flavored bouillon granules
¼   cup dried parsley flakes
2   tablespoons dried basil
1   tablespoon each dried oregano, and marjoram
1   teaspoon garlic powder
1   teaspoon ground black pepper

Combine all the ingredients and divide into 4 equal portions. Seal in 4 separate bags.

Bag # 2

1   lb. bag dried navy beans or great northern beans
1   lb. bag dried red kidney beans

Combine the beans and divide into 4 equal portions. Seal in 4 separate bags.

Bag # 3

4   cups dry elbow macaroni

Divide the macaroni into 4 (1 cup) portions and seal in 4 separate bags.

Recipe for completing:

3   quarts water
⅔   cup chopped ham or one 5 oz. can chunk style ham, undrained and chopped
1   (14½ oz.) can stewed tomatoes, undrained
Contents of the bags

Sort and wash the contents of bag #2. Place in a large stockpot. Cover with water and soak overnight. Drain and add the 3 quarts of fresh water plus the contents of bag #1 and the ham. Bring to a boil, reduce heat, cover, and simmer for about 2 hours, stirring occasionally. Add the tomatoes and the contents of bag #3. Cook an additional 20 to 30 minutes or until the macaroni is tender. Serve with cornbread muffins. Refrigerate or freeze any leftovers. (8 to 10 servings)

QUICK BEAN AND PASTA SOUP

Recipe for the bag:

1   cup dried elbow macaroni
¼   cup instant potato flakes
2   tablespoons dried vegetable flakes
2   tablespoons dried chopped onions
2   tablespoons dried chopped celery flakes
1   teaspoon dried parsley flakes
1   teaspoon dried basil leaves
1   teaspoon dried oregano leaves
¼   teaspoon garlic powder
⅛   teaspoon black pepper

Mix all the ingredients and store in a plastic bag.

Recipe for completing:

1   (14 ½ oz.) can stewed tomatoes, undrained
1   (15 oz.) can great northern beans, undrained
1   (15 oz.) can red kidney beans, undrained
1   (5 oz.) can chunk style ham, undrained but chopped
3   cups water
Contents of the bag

Mix all the liquid ingredients in a large stockpot. Bring to a boil. Stir in the contents of the bag. Reduce heat and simmer, covered, for about 30 minutes. (8 to 10 servings)

ASSORTED BEAN SOUP
Recipe for the bag:

Bag # 1

1   lb. bag each of the following:
     Pinto beans, navy beans, great northern beans,
     black eyed peas, baby lima beans, large lima beans,
     red kidney beans, black beans, green split peas,
     yellow split peas, field peas, lentils, and cranberry
     beans.

Mix the beans and peas and divide into 2 cup portions. Seal in
plastic bags. (makes about 14 packages)

Bag # 2

1   cup chopped dried onions
⅓   cup salt
3   tablespoons minced dried garlic
3   tablespoons chili powder
1   tablespoon black pepper

Mix the ingredients and divide into 2 tablespoon portions. Seal
in plastic bags. (Makes about 14 packages)

Recipe for completing:

1   ham bone or 1 (5 oz.) can chunk style ham plus 1/3
      cup vegetable oil
1   (16 oz.) can stewed tomatoes, undrained
2   quarts water
Contents of both bags

Sort and wash the beans. (bag #1) Place in a large stockpot.
Cover with water and soak overnight. Drain beans. Add the 2
quarts of water, contents of bag # 2 and the ham bone or
canned ham and oil. Bring to a boil. Reduce heat and simmer,
covered, for 1½ hours. Add the stewed tomatoes and simmer an
additional 30 minutes or until the beans are cooked. Remove
the ham bone (if using) and serve. Refrigerate or freeze leftovers. Makes 2½ quarts of soup.

GRAB A BAG

LIMA BEAN SOUP

Recipe for the bag:

2   tablespoons chopped dried onions
1   tablespoon chicken flavored bouillon granules
1   teaspoon granulated brown sugar
1   teaspoon dried basil leaves
1   teaspoon dried parsley flakes
1   teaspoon mustard powder
½   teaspoon garlic powder
½   teaspoon celery salt
⅛   teaspoon white pepper

Mix all the ingredients and store in a plastic bag.

Recipe for completing:

2   (15 oz.) cans dried lima beans, undrained
1   (10 ¾ oz.) can condensed tomato soup
1   soup can of water
Contents of the bag

Combine all the ingredients in a large pot. Cover and simmer for several hours or transfer to a crock-pot and cook on low for 1 ½ to 2 hours.   (4 to 6 servings)

NAVY BEAN SOUP

Recipe for the bag:

½   cup instant potato flakes
3   tablespoons chopped dried onions
3   tablespoons dried celery flakes
3   tablespoons dried parsley flakes
1   teaspoon dried minced garlic

Mix all the ingredients and store in a plastic bag.

Recipe for completing:

2   (15 oz.) cans navy beans, undrained
1   (5 oz.) can chunk style ham, drained and chopped
1   cup water or chicken broth
Contents of the bag

Mix all the ingredients. Put in a crock-pot and cook on low for 4 to 5 hours. (4 to 6 servings)

BEAN AND CABBAGE SOUP

Recipe for the bag:

2	tablespoons chopped dried onions
1	tablespoon butter flavored granules
1	tablespoon chicken bouillon granules
1	tablespoon dried parsley flakes
1	tablespoon dried celery leaves
2	teaspoons cornstarch
1	teaspoon granulated brown sugar
½	teaspoon white pepper
¼	teaspoon caraway seeds

Combine all the ingredients and store in a small plastic bag.

Recipe for completing:

1	(14 ½ oz.) can tomatoes with garlic and onion, undrained
1	tomato can of water
1	large carrot, grated (½ cup)
2	cups chopped green cabbage
1	(15.8 oz.) can great northern beans, undrained
1	tablespoon extra light olive oil
1	tablespoon natural rice vinegar
	Contents of the bag

In a large pot combine all the ingredients. Bring to a boil. Reduce heat, cover, and simmer for 30 minutes. (Serves 4 to 6)

CROCK-POT HOT N' SPICY BEAN SOUP

Recipe for the bag:

2	tablespoons potato flakes
2	tablespoons dried minced onion
1	tablespoon cornstarch
1	teaspoon chili powder
1	teaspoon paprika
1	teaspoon mustard powder
½	teaspoon dried oregano leaves
½	teaspoon ground cumin
½	teaspoon ground coriander
½	teaspoon granulated white sugar
¼	teaspoon cayenne pepper
¼	teaspoon dried minced garlic
¼	teaspoon dried crushed red pepper flakes

Combine all the ingredients and store in a plastic bag.

Recipe for completing:

1	(16 oz.) can red kidney beans, undrained
1	(15 ½ oz.) can black beans, undrained
1	(15 oz.) can pinto beans, undrained
1	(14 ½ oz.) can Mexican tomatoes, undrained (for a less hot and spicy soup, use regular stewed tomatoes)
1	(5 oz.) can chunk style ham, undrained but chopped
1	cup water
	Contents of the bag

Combine all the ingredients in a crock-pot. Stir well to mix. Cook on low for 9 hours. Serve as soup or serve over rice. (8 to 10 servings)

MEXICAN SOUP

Recipe for the bag:

3   tablespoons taco seasoning mix found in the ET
    CETERA section of this book (you may use a
    package of premixed taco seasoning)
2   tablespoons dried chopped onions

Mix the ingredients and store in a small plastic bag.

Recipe for completing:

1   lb. ground beef
1   (15 oz.) can pinto beans, undrained
1   bean can of spicy tomato juice
1   (4 oz.) can chopped mild green chili peppers,
    undrained
    Contents of the bag

Brown the ground beef until it is no longer pink. Drain off the fat.
Stir in the contents of the bag, chili peppers, pinto beans (mash
some of the beans as you stir.) Gradually add the tomato juice,
cover, and simmer for 15 to 20 minutes. Serve with crackers,
cornbread, or corn chips. (4 servings)

CHICKEN STEW OLÉ

Recipe for the bag:

1	tablespoon cornstarch
1	tablespoon dried chopped chives
1	tablespoon chicken flavored bouillon granules
1	teaspoon garlic powder
1	teaspoon ground cumin
1	teaspoon dried oregano leaves
1	teaspoon chili powder
1	teaspoon salt
½	teaspoon black pepper
¼	teaspoon dried crushed red pepper flakes

Combine all the ingredients and store in a plastic bag.

Recipe for completing:

1	(16 oz.) can refried beans
1	(15 oz.) can pinto beans with onions, undrained
1	(14 oz.) can corn with green peppers, undrained
1	(4 oz.) can chopped green chili peppers, undrained
1	(10 oz.) can chunk style chicken, undrained (shredded or chopped)
1	cup water
	Contents of the bag

Mix the water, a little at the time, with the refried beans to make a smooth paste. Add the beans, corn, and chili peppers. Bring to a boil and stir in the contents of the bag. Add the chicken and simmer for about 30 minutes. (6 servings)

ALMOST HOMEMADE CHICKEN NOODLE SOUP

Recipe for the bag:

15 to 20 linguine noodles, broken into pieces
1   tablespoon butter flavored granules
2   teaspoons chicken flavored bouillon granules
¼   teaspoon dried chopped chives
¼   teaspoon onion powder
¼   teaspoon crushed parsley flakes
⅛   teaspoon ground thyme
⅛   teaspoon white pepper

Combine all the ingredients and store in a plastic bag.

Recipe for completing:

1   (5 oz.) can chunk style white chicken, undrained
2   cups water
Contents of the bag

Bring the water to a boil in a medium saucepan. Stir in the contents of the bag. Return to a boil, reduce heat, and cook uncovered for 10 minutes or until noodles are tender. Stir in the chicken, cover, and heat for 5 more minutes. Serve hot. (2 servings)

SPICY SAUSAGE STEW

Recipe for the bag:

2   tablespoons dried chopped onions
1   teaspoon chili powder
1   teaspoon paprika
1   teaspoon ground cumin
½   teaspoon dried minced garlic
½   teaspoon granulated white sugar
½   teaspoon granulated brown sugar
¼   teaspoon black pepper
⅛   teaspoon cayenne pepper

Combine all the ingredients and store in a plastic bag.

Recipe for completing:

1   (12 oz.) package ground turkey or pork sausage
    (may use the 50 % less fat variety)
1   (14 ½ oz.) can Mexican style stewed tomatoes,
    undrained
1   (8 oz.) can tomato sauce
½   cup water
1   tablespoon olive oil
Contents of the bag

Brown the sausage in the olive oil. Stir and break up the sausage as you cook. Use a heavy skillet for browning over medium heat. When the sausage is no longer pink, stir in the contents of the bag. Add the tomatoes, tomato sauce, and the water. Bring to a boil. Reduce heat and simmer, covered, for 30 to 40 minutes. Serve over hot grits, rice, or noodles. (4 servings)

SAUSAGE CHOWDER

Recipe for the bag:

3 tablespoons dried chopped onions
2 tablespoons dried sweet pepper flakes
2 tablespoons dried celery flakes
1 teaspoon mustard powder
1 teaspoon salt
1 teaspoon garlic powder
1 teaspoon chili powder
1 teaspoon ground thyme
¼ teaspoon white pepper
¼ teaspoon paprika
2 packages beef flavored low sodium bouillon (about 1 tablespoon)

Mix all the ingredients and store in a plastic bag.

Recipe for completing:

1 (16 oz.) roll of mild pork sausage
2 (15 oz.) cans pinto beans, undrained
2 (14 ½ oz.) cans stewed tomatoes, undrained
1 (15 ½ oz.) can creamed style corn
Contents of the bag

Brown the sausage until no longer pink. Drain off any fat. Stir in the contents of the bag. Add the corn, beans, and the tomatoes. Bring to a boil while stirring. Reduce the heat, cover, and simmer for 1 hour. (8 servings)

SAUSAGE GUMBO

Recipe for the bag:

1   cup rice
1   tablespoon dried sweet bell pepper flakes
1   tablespoon beef flavored bouillon granules
1   tablespoon dried celery flakes
1   teaspoon paprika
1   teaspoon granulated white sugar
1   teaspoon garlic powder
1   teaspoon mustard powder
½   teaspoon black pepper
½   teaspoon gumbo file' powder
¼   teaspoon cayenne pepper
¼   teaspoon salt

Combine all the ingredients and store in a plastic bag.

Recipe for completing:

1   (14 ½ oz.) can stewed tomatoes, chopped
1   (8 oz.) can tomato sauce
1   (14 ½ oz.) can okra, drained
2   tomato cans of water (about 2 ¾ cups)
1   (14 oz.) package smoked sausage (sliced into ¼ inch
      pieces, may use low fat sausage)
Contents of the bag

Combine the water, tomatoes, okra, tomato sauce, and the
sliced sausage in a large pot. Bring to a boil. Stir in the contents of the bag. Reduce heat and simmer, covered, for about
30 minutes, stirring occasionally. Serve with cornbread. (4
servings)

HEARTY CHICKEN POTATO SOUP

Recipe for the bag:

2   tablespoons dried minced onions
1   tablespoon all purpose flour
1   tablespoon chicken flavored bouillon granules
1   teaspoon dried chopped chives
¼   teaspoon celery salt
¼   teaspoon garlic powder
⅛   teaspoon white pepper

Combine all the ingredients and store in a plastic bag.

Recipe for completing:

2   medium potatoes, peeled and cubed (about 2 ½ cups)
2   cups water
1   (12 oz.) can evaporated milk (may use skimmed)
1   (5 oz.) can chunk style chicken, chopped or shredded
2   tablespoons butter or margarine
Shredded cheddar cheese
Real bacon pieces (may use the lower fat variety)
Contents of the bag

Combine the cubed potatoes, water, butter or margarine and the contents of the bag. Bring to a boil. Reduce heat and cook, uncovered, for about 15 to 20 minutes, stirring often. With a potato masher or fork, mash some of the potatoes. Leave some of the cubes whole. Gradually stir in the milk and then add the chicken. Return to a boil, then reduce the heat and simmer for 5 to 10 more minutes. Ladle into soup bowls and top with a little cheese and bacon pieces. Serve with crackers or cornbread. (4 servings)

WINTER WARMER (INSTANT POTATO SOUP)

Recipe for the bag:

4   cups instant potato flakes
2   cups instant non-fat dry milk
4   tablespoons dried chopped onions
4   tablespoons butter flavored granules
1   tablespoon dried chopped chives
1   tablespoon dried parsley flakes
4   teaspoons chicken flavored bouillon granules or 3
     packets low sodium chicken flavored bouillon powder
½   teaspoon celery salt
½   teaspoon white pepper

Combine all the ingredients in a large container. Divide into 1 cup portions and seal in plastic bags. (Makes about 5 ½ cups of soup mix)

Recipe for completing:

1   cup potato soup mix
1   cup milk
1   cup water

Mix the milk and the water in a medium saucepan. Stir in the potato soup mix and heat thoroughly. Stir continuously while the mixture heats and thickens. You may have to add a little more milk if the soup mixture seems too thick. Sprinkle with shredded cheddar cheese and chopped green onions, if desired. (Makes 2 cups soup)

OYSTER STEW OR SALMON CHOWDER

Recipe for the bag:

The contents of the bag are the same as the recipe for the bag for the Winter Warmer (instant potato soup) in this section of the cookbook. Store in a plastic bag as you do for the Winter Warmer.

Recipe for completing:

1½   cups milk
1   cup water
½   pint of fresh oysters plus the liquor or juice or 1 (6 1/8 oz.) can of skinless, boneless pink salmon (chunk style in spring water) undrained but flaked
Contents of the bag

Mix the milk and the water in a medium saucepan. Heat until mixture almost reaches the boiling point, stirring constantly. Do not boil. Add the contents of the bag and then the oysters or salmon. Continue to cook and stir until the oysters curl or the salmon is thoroughly heated. (4 servings)

RIBBON SOUP

Recipe for the bag:

1½   cups uncooked yoke free egg noodle ribbons
2   tablespoons chicken bouillon granules
2   tablespoons instant potato flakes
1   tablespoon butter flavored granules
2   teaspoons dried minced onions
1   teaspoon dried chopped chives
1   teaspoon dried parsley flakes
⅛   teaspoon garlic powder
⅛   teaspoon Beau Monde seasoning

Combine all the ingredients and store in a plastic bag.

Recipe for completing:

4   cups water
1   (5 oz.) can chunk style chicken, undrained and
       chopped or shredded
Contents of the bag

Bring the water to a boil in a medium saucepan. Stir in the
contents of the bag. Add the chicken. Return to a boil. Boil,
uncovered, for 7 to 8 minutes, stirring occasionally. Serve hot
with crackers. (2 to 3 servings)

VERY VEGETABLE SOUP

Recipe for the bag:

¼   cup instant potato flakes
2   tablespoons dried minced onions
1   tablespoon corn starch
1   teaspoon granulated white sugar
1   teaspoon salt
½   teaspoon ground black pepper

Combine all the ingredients and store in a plastic bag.

Recipe for completing:

2   (14½ oz.) cans stewed tomatoes, undrained
1   (15 oz.) can whole kernel yellow corn, undrained
1   (15 oz.) can Lima beans, undrained
1   (14½ oz.) can cut okra, drained
2   cups shredded cabbage
1   cup water
½   cup milk
2   tablespoons corn oil
Contents of the bag

Empty the contents of the cans into a large pot. Add the water, corn oil, and cabbage. Bring to a boil, lower the heat, and simmer for 15 minutes. Stir the pot several times. Add the milk to the contents of the bag. Gradually add this mixture to the soup stirring as you pour. Simmer another 15 minutes, stirring often. Serve hot with cornbread muffins. (4 to 6 servings)

MAIN DISH

GRAB A BAG

MAIN DISH

CURRIED ALFREDO LINGUINE

Recipe for the bag:

1	tablespoon butter flavored granules
1	tablespoon chicken flavored bouillon granules
1	tablespoon cornstarch
2	teaspoons dried parsley flakes
1	teaspoon dried chopped chives
¼	teaspoon garlic powder
¼	teaspoon onion powder
⅛	teaspoon white pepper
⅛	teaspoon curry powder

Combine all the ingredients and store in a plastic bag.

Recipe for completing:

1	(8 oz.) package of linguine
1	cup hot water
½	cup sour cream
⅓	cup grated Parmesan cheese
	Contents of the bag

Cook linguine according to package directions. While the pasta is cooking, combine the water and the contents of the bag in a medium saucepan. Bring to a boil and stir until thickened. Remove from heat and cool. Whisk sour cream into cooled sauce. Combine with the drained and rinsed linguine. Sprinkle on the cheese and serve hot. (4 servings)

BLACK BEANS WITH RICE

Recipe for the bag:

1   cup rice
2   tablespoons dried chopped onions
1   tablespoon butter flavored granules
¼   teaspoon dried minced garlic
¼   teaspoon dried basil leaves
¼   teaspoon dried oregano leaves
¼   teaspoon dried parsley flakes
¼   teaspoon dried crushed red pepper flakes

Combine all the ingredients and store in a plastic bag.

Recipe for completing:

1   (15 oz.) can black beans, undrained
1   (5 oz.) can chunk style ham, undrained and chopped
2   cups water
Contents of the bag

Place the beans, water, and ham in a medium pot and bring to a boil. Stir in the contents of the bag and mix well. Return to a boil, cover, and reduce heat. Simmer for about 20 minutes or until thoroughly heated and rice is tender. Serve with cornbread. (4 to 6 servings)

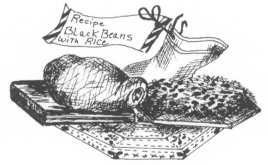

CHINESE CHICKEN AND VEGETABLES

Recipe for the bag:

2	tablespoons cornstarch
1	tablespoon dried minced onions
½	teaspoon white granulated sugar
½	teaspoon salt
⅛	teaspoon ground ginger
⅛	teaspoon garlic powder
⅛	teaspoon curry powder
⅛	teaspoon cayenne pepper
⅛	teaspoon black pepper

Combine all the ingredients and store in a plastic bag.

Recipe for completing:

1	cup water
¼	cup olive oil
¼	cup soy sauce (may use the lite, low sodium variety)
1	tablespoon cooking sherry
1	lb. boneless chicken (cut into 1" strips)
5 or 6	stalks of fresh asparagus (cut into 1" pieces)
1	bunch of green onions (cut into 1" pieces)
1	(6 oz.) package frozen pea pods
1	(8 oz.) can sliced water chestnuts, drained
1	(8 oz.) can bamboo shoots, drained

Contents of the bag

Combine the water, soy sauce, cooking sherry, and the contents of the bag. Mix well and set aside. Brown the chicken strips in the olive oil. After the chicken begins to cook, stir in the asparagus, onions, water chestnuts, bamboo shoots and the frozen pea pods. Cook and stir for 5 or 6 minutes or until the chicken is no longer pink. Stir in the soy mixture and continue to cook and stir until thickened. Serve over hot cooked rice and chow mein noodles. (6 servings)

EASY CHICKEN POT PIE
Recipe for the bag:

Bag # 1

2 tablespoons dried minced onions
1 tablespoon chicken flavored bouillon granules
¼ teaspoon celery salt
¼ teaspoon black pepper
⅛ teaspoon ground sage
⅛ teaspoon curry powder

Bag # 2

1 cup self-rising flour
½ cup non-fat dry milk
¼ teaspoon salt
¼ teaspoon white pepper

Combine the ingredients for the bags separately and store in 2 individual plastic bags.

Recipe for completing:

1 (10 ¾ oz.) can cream of chicken soup or cream of mushroom soup
1 (8.5 oz.) can small green peas, undrained
1 (10 oz.) can chunk style chicken (white meat 98% fat-free) undrained
1 stick butter or margarine, melted
2 cups water

Mix together the chicken, soup, peas, 1 cup of the water, and the contents of bag # 1. Spread into a greased 11 inches x 8 inches x 1 ½ inches baking dish. Mix together the remaining cup of water and the melted margarine or butter. Gradually add the contents of bag # 2, stirring until no lumps appear. Pour over the chicken mixture. Bake at 400 degrees for 45 to 60 minutes or until the crust is lightly browned and the liquid is almost absorbed. (4 to 6 servings)

CHICKEN AND RICE FOR TWO

Recipe for the bag:

Bag # 1

½ cup rice
1 tablespoon butter flavored granules

Combine the ingredients and store in a plastic bag.

Bag # 2

2 tablespoons dried minced onions
1 (0.19 oz.) package or ½ tablespoon instant chicken
   flavored bouillon granules or powder
¼ teaspoon onion powder
¼ teaspoon celery salt
¼ teaspoon ground sage
¼ teaspoon crushed dried parsley flakes
⅛ teaspoon white pepper
⅛ teaspoon curry powder

Combine all the ingredients and store in a plastic bag.

Recipe for completing:

1 chicken breast (2 pieces)
1 (10 ¾ oz.) can cream of chicken soup
½ soup can of water
Contents of both bags
Olive oil cooking spray

Coat an 8" x 8" x 2" baking dish or pan with the olive oil cooking spray. Combine the soup and the water and stir until smooth. Divide the soup mixture into 2 equal portions. Add the contents of bag # 1 to one portion and the contents of bag # 2 to the other portion. Place the rice mixture (bag # 1) in the prepared dish or pan. Lay the chicken pieces over the top. Pour the remaining mixture (bag # 2) over the chicken. Cover the dish or pan with aluminum foil and bake at 350 degrees for 45 minutes. (serves 2)

NO FUSS FAJITAS

Recipe for the bag:

1	tablespoon dried celery flakes
1	tablespoon dried sweet bell pepper flakes
1	tablespoon dried minced onions
1	tablespoon chili powder
1	teaspoon garlic powder
1	teaspoon onion powder
1	teaspoon seasoned salt
½	teaspoon black pepper

Combine all the ingredients and store in a large resealable plastic bag.

Recipe for completing:

1	lb. chicken breast or chicken tenders, cut across the grain into ¼ " strips
2	tablespoons olive oil
8	(6 inch) flour tortillas

Juice from 1 lime
Contents of the bag
Toppings of choice such as chopped green onions, chopped
tomatoes, salsa, sour cream, guacamole or shredded
Mexican cheese

Add chicken to the contents of the bag. Shake to coat. Heat oil in a skillet. Add the coated chicken. Cook and stir until the chicken is no longer pink. (5 to 10 minutes) Squeeze on the lime juice. Heat the tortillas, according to package directions. Let each person assemble his or her own fajita. Spoon on chicken mixture and top as you choose.
(4 to 6 servings)

TERIYAKI CHICKEN

Recipe for the bag:

2   tablespoons granulated brown sugar
1   tablespoon dried chopped onions
½   teaspoon ground ginger
⅛   teaspoon dried minced garlic
⅛   teaspoon mustard powder
⅛   teaspoon black pepper
⅛   teaspoon curry powder

Combine all the ingredients and store in a plastic bag.

Recipe for completing:

4   chicken breasts, skin removed
½   cup soy sauce
¼   cup rice vinegar
¼   cup olive oil
Contents of the bag

Combine the soy sauce, vinegar, and the olive oil. Stir in the contents of the bag. Place the chicken in a shallow container. Pour the mixture over the chicken. Cover and marinate in the refrigerator overnight. Turn several times. When ready to use, remove the chicken from the mixture and grill over medium coals until done. Baste with the leftover marinade, as the chicken cooks. (4 servings)

MEXICAN MEAT LOAF

Recipe for the bag:

½   cup cracker crumbs
1   tablespoon dried chopped onions
1   tablespoon dried sweet bell pepper flakes
1   tablespoon chili powder
1   teaspoon dried cilantro flakes
1   teaspoon ground cumin
1   teaspoon dried oregano leaves
1   teaspoon dried basil leaves
½   teaspoon garlic powder
⅛   teaspoon cayenne pepper

Combine all the ingredients and store in a plastic bag.

Recipe for completing:

1½   lbs. lean ground beef
1   egg, beaten
1   (8 oz.) can tomato sauce
¼   cup tomato catsup
Contents of the bag

Mix all the ingredients, reserving ½ of the tomato sauce. Use
your hands and mix well. Shape into a loaf and place in a baking
dish or pan. Pour the remaining tomato sauce over the top. Bake
at 350 degrees for about 45 minutes. (6 to 8 servings)

CAPTIVATING RICE CASSEROLE

Recipe for the bag:

2   cups long grain white rice
2   tablespoons butter flavored granules
2   tablespoons dried chopped onions
2   teaspoons dried parsley flakes
2   teaspoons dried basil leaves
½   teaspoon garlic powder
½   teaspoon ground poultry seasoning or sage

Mix all the ingredients and store in a plastic bag.

Recipe for completing:

2   (10 ¾ oz.) cans cream of chicken-mushroom soup
    or 1 can of cream of chicken soup and 1 can of cream
    of mushroom soup
1   (10 ¾ oz.) can French onion soup
1   (4 oz.) can sliced mushrooms, undrained
1   soup can of water
1½ cups chopped leftover cooked chicken or turkey
Contents of the bag

Empty the soups, sliced mushrooms, and the water in a large container. Stir in the contents of the bag and chopped chicken or turkey. Pour into a 13" x 9" x 2" casserole dish or pan. Cover and bake at 350 degrees for 1 hour and 15 minutes or until the rice is tender. For a side dish , omit the chicken or turkey. This is a good way to use leftover chicken or turkey. (8 to 10 servings)

PESTO AND PASTA

Recipe for the bag:

4   tablespoons instant non-fat dry milk
2   teaspoons dried basil leaves
1   teaspoon dried parsley flakes
1   teaspoon butter flavored granules
½   teaspoon celery salt
½   teaspoon onion salt
½   teaspoon garlic powder
½   teaspoon ground oregano

Mix all the ingredients and seal in a plastic bag.

Recipe for completing:

1   (8 oz.) package of fettuccini
2   tablespoons water
2   tablespoons olive oil
2   tablespoons Parmesan cheese
Contents of the bag

Drop the fettuccini into boiling water and cook for 8 to 11 minutes. Drain and rinse with hot water. Combine the contents of the bag with the 2 tablespoons of water and the olive oil. Let the mixture sit while the pasta is cooking. Put the drained pasta in a shallow dish. Pour the pesto mixture over the pasta and toss. Sprinkle on the Parmesan cheese and toss again. Serve immediately. (4 servings)

BAKED PORK CHOPS

Recipe for the bag:

1	tablespoon cornstarch
½	teaspoon paprika
½	teaspoon onion powder
½	teaspoon caraway seed
½	teaspoon dried dill weed
⅛	teaspoon garlic powder
⅛	teaspoon white pepper

Combine all the ingredients and store in a plastic bag.

Recipe for completing:

4	lean pork chops or pork loins
1	tablespoon cooking oil
¾	cup water
	Contents of the bag

Brown the pork chops or loins on each side in the oil in a medium skillet. When brown, lift out and place in an 8" x 8" x 2" baking dish. Preheat the oven to 350 degrees. Add the contents of the bag to the water. Stir well. Pour over the pork chops or loins. Cover and bake for 1 hour. (4 servings)

TUNA AND BROCCOLI WITH CORNBREAD

Recipe for the bag:

½ teaspoon ground sage
¼ teaspoon mustard powder
¼ teaspoon paprika
¼ teaspoon onion powder

Mix all the ingredients and store in a small plastic bag.

Recipe for completing:

2 (10 oz.) packages frozen broccoli spears
1 cup boiling water
2 (6½ oz.) cans tuna, drained and flaked
2 (10¾ oz.) cans cream of mushroom soup
1 package corn muffin mix
Contents of the bag

Heat the oven to 400 degrees. Cook the broccoli in the boiling water for about 5 minutes. Drain. Arrange the broccoli in a 13" x 9" x 2" casserole dish. Cover with the flaked tuna. Prepare the muffin mix according to package directions. Heat the undiluted mushroom soup and stir in the contents of the bag. Spread the soup mixture over the tuna and broccoli. Drop the prepared muffin mix by tablespoons over the hot soup. Bake for 30 to 35 minutes or until the cornbread is golden brown. (8 to 10 servings)

TUNA NOODLE CASSEROLE

Recipe for the bag

3 tablespoons instant non-fat dry milk
2 tablespoons dried celery flakes
1 tablespoon cornstarch
1 tablespoon dried parsley flakes
1 tablespoon butter flavored granules
1 tablespoon dried chopped onions
½ teaspoon garlic powder
½ teaspoon onion salt
½ teaspoon celery salt
⅛ teaspoon white pepper

Mix all the ingredients and seal in a plastic bag.

Recipe for completing:

1 (8 oz.) package of egg noodles, cooked and drained
½ cup hot water
1 (16 ½ oz.) can early peas with pearl onions and sliced mushrooms, undrained
1 (2 oz.) bag sour cream and onion potato chips, crushed
Contents of the bag

Empty the contents of the bag into the hot water. Stir well and let sit while the egg noodles are cooking. Drain and rinse the noodles. Combine with all the ingredients except the crushed chips. Place in a two-quart casserole dish. Top with the crushed chips. Bake at 350 degrees for 20 to 30 minutes. (4 to 6 servings)

OVEN FRIED FLOUNDER

Recipe for the bag:

½   cup cornmeal mix
½   cup biscuit mix
¼   cup Parmesan cheese
1   teaspoon onion powder
½   teaspoon salt
½   teaspoon lemon pepper
¼   teaspoon garlic powder
¼   teaspoon dried parsley flakes
¼   teaspoon dried oregano leaves
¼   teaspoon dried basil leaves

Mix all the ingredients and store in a plastic bag.

Recipe for completing:

1   (10 oz.) package frozen flounder
½   stick butter or margarine
Contents of the bag

Thaw the flounder. Separate the fillets. Melt the margarine or butter in a roasting pan. Rinse the fish. Coat the fish with the contents of the bag. Put the coated fish in the roasting pan on top of the melted butter or margarine, in a single layer. Bake, uncovered, at 350 degrees for 20 to 25 minutes. Turn once and continue baking for about 15 more minutes or until fish is done. (4 servings)

JAMBALAYA

Recipe for the bag:

4   cups long grain white rice
1   cup dried sweet bell pepper flakes
1   cup dried celery flakes
¼   cup dried chopped onions
¼   cup dried parsley flakes
3   tablespoons beef flavored bouillon granules
1½ teaspoons paprika
1   teaspoon cayenne pepper
1   teaspoon dried minced garlic
1   teaspoon ground cumin
1   teaspoon dried thyme leaves
1   teaspoon dried oregano leaves
1   teaspoon dried basil leaves
1   teaspoon gumbo file'

Combine all the ingredients in a large container. Divide into 4 equal portions. (about 1 ⅔ cups) Seal in 4 separate plastic bags.

Recipe for completing:

1   (16 oz.) package kielbasa or other smoked sausage (cut into ¼" slices)
1   (14 ½ oz.) can Cajun or Mexican style stewed tomatoes, undrained
 2¼ cups water
Contents of one bag

In a large skillet or pot, combine the sausage, water, tomatoes, and the contents of one bag. Bring to a boil. Stir several times, cover, reduce heat, and simmer for about 20 minutes. Serve hot. (6 to 8 servings)

SHRIMP CREOLE

Recipe for the bag:

2	tablespoons self-rising flour
2	tablespoons dried chopped onions
1	tablespoon beef flavored bouillon granules
1	tablespoon dried sweet bell pepper flakes
1	tablespoon dried celery flakes
1	teaspoon garlic powder
1	teaspoon dried basil leaves
1	teaspoon dried thyme leaves
1	teaspoon chili powder
1	teaspoon white granulated sugar
1	teaspoon salt
¼	teaspoon black pepper
¼	teaspoon cayenne pepper
¼	teaspoon ground sage
2	bay leaves

Mix all the ingredients and store in a plastic bag.

Recipe for completing:

½	stick butter or margarine
2	(5 oz.) cans shrimp, drained
1	(14 ½ oz.) can Cajun or Mexican style stewed tomatoes, undrained
1	cup water
	Contents of the bag

Melt the margarine in a medium skillet. Stir in the contents of the bag. Add the tomatoes and the water. Stir until thickened. Just before serving, stir in the shrimp. When the shrimp are heated thoroughly, serve over hot cooked rice or noodles. (4 to 6 servings)

SALMON FETTUCCINI

Recipe for the bag:

2   tablespoons dry non-fat milk
2   tablespoons dried chopped onions
2   tablespoons butter flavored granules
1   tablespoon instant potato flakes
½   teaspoon dried parsley flakes
½   teaspoon garlic powder
½   teaspoon celery salt
½   teaspoon dried dill weed
⅛   teaspoon white pepper

Mix all the ingredients and store in a plastic bag.

Recipe for completing:

1   (6 oz.) package fettuccini, cooked and rinsed
1   (8 ½ oz.) can peas and carrots, drained but with
    liquid reserved
1   (6 ¼ oz.) can chunk style salmon in spring water,
    drained and flaked
1   cup milk
½   cup sour cream
4   tablespoons Parmesan cheese
Contents of the bag

In a small saucepan or skillet, heat the reserved liquid from the peas and carrots. Stir in the contents of the bag. Gradually add the milk, stirring as you pour. When the mixture begins to thicken, add the salmon, peas, and carrots. Fold in the sour cream. Serve over the cooked fettuccini and sprinkle with the Parmesan cheese. Serve immediately. (2 to 4 servings)

SHRIMP AND SAUSAGE SKILLET

Recipe for the bag:

1   cup long grain white rice
2   tablespoons dried chopped onions
1   tablespoon dried celery flakes
1   tablespoon dried sweet bell pepper flakes
1   tablespoon dried chopped chives or green onions
1½ teaspoons seafood seasoning
1   teaspoon dried minced garlic

Mix all the ingredients and seal in a plastic bag.

Recipe for completing:

1   lb. small to medium raw shrimp (peeled, cleaned, and washed)
1   lb. roll pork sausage (hot or mild)
2   cups water
Contents of the bag

In a heavy saucepan, bring the water to a boil. Add the contents of the bag. Cover and lower heat. Simmer 20 minutes or until the rice is tender and the water is absorbed. You will have about 3 cups of seasoned rice. While the rice is cooking, brown the sausage, chopping as you stir, much the same as you would when cooking ground beef. When browned, drain off any fat. Add the shrimp. Stir until cooked (about 5 minutes). The shrimp will turn pink. Spoon in the cooked seasoned rice and mix well. Let sit a few minutes until the rice absorbs some of the juices. Salt and pepper to taste. Serve with hush puppies. (6 to 8 servings)

ITALIAN BEEF AND MACARONI

Recipe for the bag:

2   cups dry elbow macaroni
2   tablespoons dried chopped onions
2   teaspoons chili powder
1   teaspoon dried Italian seasoning
½   teaspoon onion salt
½   teaspoon celery salt

Mix all the ingredients and store in a plastic bag.

Recipe for completing:

1   lb. ground beef
1½ cups water
1   (14½ oz.) can Italian stewed tomatoes, undrained
Contents of the bag

Brown the ground beef in a medium skillet. Drain off any fat. Add the remaining ingredients. Bring to a boil, while stirring. Reduce the heat and cook for 20 to 25 minutes or until the macaroni is tender. Stir occasionally and add additional water, if needed. (Serves 4 to 6)

CANCUN CASSEROLE

Recipe for the bag:

¼ cup long grain white rice
1 (1¼ oz.) package taco seasoning mix or 3 tablespoons taco seasoning mix found in the ET CETERA section of this cookbook

Mix and seal in a plastic bag.

Recipe for completing:

1 lb. ground beef
1 cup water
1 (14½ oz.) can Mexican style stewed tomatoes, undrained
1 (15½ oz.) can pinto beans, undrained
1 cup shredded Mexican cheese mix or use cheddar
1 cup crushed tortilla chips
Contents of the bag

Brown the ground beef in a large skillet. Drain off any fat. Add all the other ingredients except the cheese and chips. Stir well. Empty the mixture into a 13" x 9" x 2" casserole dish. Cover and bake at 350 degrees for about 40 minutes. Remove cover. Sprinkle the crushed chips over the casserole and then the shredded cheese. Return to the oven for 5 to 10 minutes or until the cheese melts. (Serves 4 to 6)

SPAGHETTI SAUCE

Recipe for the bag:

1½ tablespoons dried chopped onions
1½ tablespoons dried sweet bell pepper flakes
1½ tablespoons dried celery flakes
2   teaspoons dried basil leaves
1   teaspoon dried oregano leaves
1   teaspoon dried parsley flakes
1   teaspoon dried Italian seasoning
1   teaspoon garlic powder
1   teaspoon chili powder
1   teaspoon paprika

Mix all the ingredients and store in a plastic bag.

Recipe for completing:

1   lb. ground beef
2   (10 oz.) cans condensed tomato soup
2   (8 oz.) cans tomato sauce
2   (6 oz.) cans tomato paste
2   soup cans of water
Contents of the bag

Brown the ground beef in a small skillet. Drain off any fat. While the beef is browning, empty all the remaining ingredients into a large pot. Stir well to mix. Add the drained ground beef and stir again. Simmer for several hours, stirring often. Serve over hot cooked spaghetti noodles. Freeze leftover sauce to use at a later date. (8 to 10 servings)

SKILLET STROGANOFF

Recipe for the bag:

2 tablespoons self-rising flour
1 tablespoon dried chopped onions
1 tablespoon low sodium beef flavored bouillon
   granules
1½ teaspoons butter flavored granules
½ teaspoon dried parsley flakes
½ teaspoon garlic powder
½ teaspoon salt
⅛ teaspoon white pepper

Mix all the ingredients and store in a plastic bag.

Recipe for completing:

1 lb. ground beef
1 (4½ oz.) jar sliced mushrooms, undrained
1 (10¾ oz.) can cream of mushroom soup
1 cup sour cream
1 (6 oz.) package of no yoke noodles, cooked
   according to the package directions and drained
Contents of the bag

Brown the ground beef. Drain off any fat. Stir in the contents of
the bag. Add the sliced mushrooms and the mushroom soup.
Stir well. Just before serving, stir in the sour cream and cooked
noodles. Serve hot. (4 to 6 servings)

WHITE CHILI

Recipe for the bag:

2   tablespoons butter flavored granules
1   tablespoon dried chopped onions
2   teaspoons celery salt
2   teaspoons ground cumin
2   teaspoons ground coriander or cilantro
½   teaspoon chili powder

Mix all the ingredients and seal in a plastic bag.

Recipe for completing:

2   (15.8 oz.) cans great northern beans, undrained
2   (10½ oz.) cans low sodium, low fat chicken broth
2   (5 oz.) cans chunk style chicken, drained and flaked
1   (4 oz.) can chopped mild green chili peppers,
    undrained
Contents of the bag

In a large stockpot, empty all the cans. Stir in the contents of the bag. Mix well. Bring to a boil, cover, reduce heat and simmer for 30 minutes, stirring several times. Serve in bowls sprinkled with shredded Swiss cheese. (6 to 8 servings)

NO MEAT CHILI

Recipe for the bag:

2	tablespoons instant potato flakes
1	tablespoon dried chopped onions
1	tablespoon dried vegetable flakes
1	tablespoon sweet bell pepper flakes
1	tablespoon granulated brown sugar
1	tablespoon chili powder
1	tablespoon beef flavored bouillon granules
1	teaspoon garlic powder
1	teaspoon ground cumin
1	teaspoon paprika
1	teaspoon ground sage
1	teaspoon dried oregano leaves
1	teaspoon dried basil leaves
1	teaspoon dried parsley flakes
1	teaspoon dried cilantro leaves
1/2	teaspoon salt
1/8	teaspoon cayenne pepper

Mix all the ingredients and store in a plastic bag.

Recipe for completing;

1	(15 1/2 oz.) can chili style stewed tomatoes, undrained
1	(16 oz.) can navy beans, undrained
1	(16 oz.) can pinto beans, undrained
1	(16 oz.) can red kidney beans, undrained
1	(6 oz.) can tomato paste
	Contents of the bag

Mix all the ingredients in a large pot. Bring to a boil. Reduce heat, cover, and simmer for 2 hours. You may cook in a crock-pot for 4 hours on low. Serve with saltine crackers. (Serves 8)

PRONTO CHILI

Recipe for the bag:

3   tablespoons paprika
2   tablespoons chili powder
2   tablespoons dried chopped onions
1   tablespoon garlic powder
1½ teaspoons ground cumin
¼   teaspoon salt
⅛   teaspoon black pepper
⅛   teaspoon ground red pepper

Mix all the ingredients and store in a plastic bag.

Recipe for completing:

2   lbs. ground beef
1   (8 oz.) can tomato sauce
1   (6 oz.) can tomato paste
2   (14 oz.) cans chili beef soup
1   (16 oz.) can pinto beans, undrained
2   cups water
Contents of the bag

Brown the ground beef. Drain off any fat. Stir in the contents of the bag. Add the water, tomato sauce, tomato paste, soup, and beans. Bring to a boil. Reduce heat, cover, and simmer for 2 to 3 hours or transfer to a crock-pot and cook on low for 3 to 4 hours. You may garnish the chili with shredded cheddar cheese and chopped onions. Serve with saltine crackers. (6 to 8 servings)

FRANKS AND RICE

Recipe for the bag:

1	cup long grain white rice
2	tablespoons dried chopped onions
1	tablespoon dried chopped chives
1	teaspoon dried minced garlic
½	teaspoon mustard powder
½	teaspoon celery salt
½	teaspoon caraway seeds
¼	teaspoon white pepper

Mix all the ingredients and store in a plastic bag.

Recipe for completing:

1	(10 oz.) can chopped kraut, drained
5	franks or wieners (cut into 1" pieces)
2	cups water
	Contents of the bag

In a large skillet, bring the water to a boil. Stir in the contents of the bag, kraut, and the franks or wieners. Reduce heat, cover, and simmer for 20 minutes or until the rice is tender. (4 servings)

OCTOBERFEST QUICKIE

Recipe for the bag:

1   tablespoon dried chopped onions
1   tablespoon butter flavored granules
1   teaspoon celery salt
1   teaspoon caraway seeds
¼   teaspoon chili powder
¼   teaspoon black pepper
¼   teaspoon garlic powder

Mix all the ingredients and store in a plastic bag.

Recipe for completing:

1   (10 oz.) can chopped kraut, drained
1   (5 oz.) can chunk style ham, undrained and flaked or
      chopped
1   (16 oz.) can small whole potatoes, undrained
Contents of the bag

In a large electric skillet, empty the kraut, ham, and the potatoes. Stir in the contents of the bag. Bring to a boil, reduce heat, and simmer for about 10 minutes or until thoroughly heated. Serve with cornbread muffins. (4 servings)

BEEF STEW IN A WINK

Recipe for the bag:

1   tablespoon dried chopped onions
1   tablespoon cornstarch
3/4 teaspoon celery salt
1/2 teaspoon garlic salt
1/4 teaspoon black pepper
1/8 teaspoon onion powder

Combine all the ingredients and seal in a plastic bag.

Recipe for completing:

1   (16 oz.) can stewed tomatoes, undrained
1   (1½ lb. or 24 oz.) can of beef stew
1   (16 oz.) can mixed vegetables, undrained
Contents of the bag

Combine the canned ingredients. Stir in the contents of the bag. Place in a pot and bring to a boil, stirring until the boil is reached. Reduce the heat and simmer, covered, for about 30 minutes. (4 to 6 servings)

RED BEANS AND RICE
Recipe for the bag:

Bag # 1
1   (16 oz.) bag dried red kidney beans

Bag # 2
1   cup long grain white rice
1   bay leaf
¼   cup dried sweet bell pepper flakes
1½   teaspoons dried chopped onions
½   teaspoon garlic powder
½   teaspoon dried oregano leaves
½   teaspoon ground thyme
½   teaspoon dried basil leaves
½   teaspoon dried parsley flakes
½   teaspoon white pepper
½   teaspoon celery salt
½   teaspoon onion powder
½   teaspoon crushed red pepper flakes
½   teaspoon granulated white sugar
½   teaspoon paprika

Combine all the ingredients and store in a plastic bag.

Recipe for completing:

1   (14½ oz.) can stewed tomatoes, undrained
1   (5 oz.) can chunk style ham, undrained and flaked or
       chopped
       Contents of both bags

Wash and sort the beans (bag # 1). Soak overnight. Drain. Put in a large pot. Add 1½ quarts of water and cook until almost done (about 1 hour). Stir in the contents of bag # 2, tomatoes, and the ham. Cook for about 20 minutes more or until the rice is cooked and most of the liquid is absorbed. Discard the bay leaf and serve. (6 to 8 servings)

QUICK RED BEANS AND RICE

Recipe for the bag:

The ingredients for the bag are the same as the regular red beans and rice (bag # 2) on the previous page.

Recipe for completing:

1 (15½ oz.) can red kidney beans, undrained
1 (14½ oz.) can stewed tomatoes, undrained
1 (5 oz.) can chunk style ham, undrained and flaked or chopped
2 cups water
   Contents of the bag

Combine all the ingredients in a medium skillet. Bring to a boil, cover, reduce heat and simmer for 30 minutes or until the rice is tender. Discard the bay leaf and serve. (4 to 6 servings)

BLACK EYED RICE

Recipe for the bag:

Bag # 1

1   (16 oz.) bag dried black eyed peas

Bag # 2

1   cup long grain white rice
2   tablespoons dried chopped onions
1   tablespoon dried celery flakes
1   teaspoon dried parsley flakes
1   teaspoon ground thyme
½   teaspoon dried rosemary
½   teaspoon salt
½   teaspoon black pepper

Combine all the ingredients for bag # 2 and store in a plastic bag.

Recipe for completing:

1   (14½ oz.) can stewed tomatoes, undrained
1   (5 oz.) can chunk style ham, undrained and chopped
Contents of both bags

Wash and sort the beans (bag # 1). Cover with water and soak overnight. Drain. Put into a large pot. Add 1½ quarts of water and cook until almost done (about 1 hour). Stir in the contents of (bag # 2), the ham, and the tomatoes. Cook 20 minutes more or until the rice and the beans are done. (6 to 8 servings)

QUICK BLACK EYED RICE

Recipe for the bag:

The ingredients for the bag are the same as for the regular black eyed rice (bag # 2) on the previous page.

Recipe for completing:

1   (14 ½ oz.) can stewed tomatoes, undrained
1   (16 oz.) can black eyed peas, undrained
1   (5 oz.) can chunk style ham, undrained and chopped
2   cups water
Contents of the bag

In a large skillet or pot, bring the water to a boil. Stir in the contents of the bag, black eyed peas, tomatoes, and the ham. Return to a boil, cover, reduce heat and simmer for 20 to 30 minutes or until the rice is cooked and liquid is almost absorbed. (6 servings)

CHILI BURGERS

Recipe for the bag:

1   tablespoon instant potato flakes
1½ teaspoons chili powder
1½ teaspoons dried chopped onions
1   teaspoon cornstarch
1   teaspoon paprika
1   teaspoon dried minced garlic
1   teaspoon ground cumin
½ teaspoon salt
½ teaspoon black pepper
½ teaspoon mustard powder

Combine all the ingredients and store in a plastic bag.

Recipe for completing:

1   lb. ground beef
1½ cups water
1   (6 oz.) can tomato paste
Contents of the bag

Brown the ground beef. Drain. Stir in the contents of the bag and the tomato paste. Add the water, a little at the time, until you have the consistency that you want. Simmer for 15 minutes. Serve on hamburger buns. (4 to 6 sandwiches)

SAVORY OVEN FRIED CHICKEN

Recipe for the bag:

1	cup plain bread crumbs
1	cup biscuit mix
1	tablespoon dried Italian seasoning
1	teaspoon garlic powder
1	teaspoon paprika
¼	teaspoon curry powder
¼	teaspoon ground poultry seasoning or sage

Mix all the ingredients and store in a plastic bag.

Recipe for completing:

2	lbs. chicken pieces, washed
2	tablespoons butter or margarine
	Contents of the bag

Preheat the oven to 425 degrees. Melt the margarine in a 13" x 9" x 2" pan in the oven. Coat the wet chicken with the contents of the bag. Place the coated chicken pieces in a single layer, in the pan, on top of the melted margarine or butter. Bake about 30 minutes.
Turn the chicken pieces and bake an additional 15 minutes or until the chicken is done.
(8 servings)

CROCK-POT CHICKEN AND BEANS

Recipe for the bag:

4   tablespoons dried vegetable flakes
4   tablespoons dried chopped onions
3   tablespoons dried celery flakes
1   tablespoon dried sweet bell pepper flakes
½   tablespoon dried minced garlic
1   bay leaf

Mix all the ingredients and seal in a plastic bag.

Recipe for completing:

2   (15 oz.) cans navy beans, drained
1   cup tomato juice
2   whole chicken breasts (4 pieces) cut into 1" strips
Contents of the bag

Combine all the ingredients in a crock-pot. Cover and cook on low heat for 8 to 10 hours. Remove and discard the bay leaf before serving. (4 servings)

BARBECUED CHICKEN IN FOIL

Recipe for the bag:

2   teaspoons salt
2   teaspoons chili powder
1   teaspoon mustard powder
1   teaspoon paprika
¼   teaspoon ground red pepper

Mix all the ingredients and seal in a plastic bag.

Recipe for completing:

2   lbs. fryer chicken, cut up
¼   cup water
3   tablespoons tomato catsup
2   tablespoons cider vinegar
2   tablespoons Worcestershire sauce
2   tablespoons melted butter or margarine
1   tablespoon lemon juice
Contents of the bag

Combine the liquid ingredients. Stir in the contents of the bag.
Dip the chicken pieces into the sauce and then arrange the
pieces in a single layer on a piece of heavy duty aluminum foil.
Spoon the remaining sauce over the chicken. Seal the foil tightly
and place in a roasting pan. Bake at 500 degrees for 15 minutes. Reduce the oven temperature to 350 degrees and continue to bake for an additional 1¼ to 1½ hours or until the
chicken is tender. (6 to 8 servings)

CHICKEN SPINACH BAKE

Recipe for the bag:

¼ cup self-rising flour
¼ teaspoon white pepper
¼ teaspoon mustard powder
¼ teaspoon onion powder
¼ teaspoon dried chopped chives
¼ teaspoon dried parsley flakes
¼ teaspoon paprika
¼ teaspoon garlic powder

Mix all the ingredients and seal in a plastic bag.

Recipe for completing:

1   stick of butter or margarine
2   cups milk
½   cup mayonnaise
1   tablespoon lemon juice
2   (5 oz.) cans chunk style chicken, drained and flaked
2   (10 oz.) packages frozen spinach, cooked and drained
1   cup croutons (crushed)
Contents of the bag

Heat the oven to 350 degrees. Melt the margarine or butter in a medium saucepan. Whisk in the contents of the bag. Cook and stir over low heat until the mixture is smooth. Slowly add the milk, stirring constantly, until the mixture is smooth and free of lumps. Boil for 1 minute. Remove from the heat and blend in the mayonnaise and lemon juice. Spread the chicken in a 10" x 6" x 1½" casserole dish. Top with half the sauce. Mix the remaining sauce with the spinach and spread over the chicken and sauce already in the dish. Sprinkle the crushed croutons over the top. Bake, uncovered, for 25 to 30 minutes. (6 servings)

QUICK BRUNSWICK STEW

Recipe for the bag:

2 packets of low sodium chicken flavored bouillon or 1
   tablespoon granules
3 tablespoons dried chopped onions
2 tablespoons instant potato flakes
1 tablespoon cornstarch
1 teaspoon granulated white sugar
1 teaspoon dried basil leaves
1 teaspoon dried oregano leaves
1/4 teaspoon paprika
1/8 teaspoon black pepper

Mix all the ingredients and seal in a plastic bag.

Recipe for completing:

2 (3 oz.) cans chunk style chicken, drained and flaked
1 (5 oz.) can chunk style ham, drained and chopped
1 (15 oz.) can lima beans, undrained
1 (15 oz.) can shoe peg corn, undrained
1 (15 oz.) can stewed tomatoes, undrained
1 (15 oz.) can low sodium chicken broth
1 broth can of water
Contents of the bag

Empty all of the canned ingredients and the can of water into a
large pot. Stir in the contents of the bag. Bring to a boil. Reduce the heat and simmer for 1 hour, stirring occasionally. (8 to
10 servings)

SKILLET RICE DINNER

Recipe for the bag:

1   cup long grain white rice
2   tablespoons dried vegetable flakes
1   tablespoon dried celery flakes
1   tablespoon dried chopped chives or green onions
1   tablespoon chicken flavored bouillon granules
1   teaspoon dried Italian seasoning

Mix all the ingredients and store in a plastic bag.

Recipe for completing:

2   cups water
1   (8½ oz.) can peas and carrots, undrained
1   (4 oz.) can sliced mushrooms, undrained
1   (3 oz.) can chunk style white chicken, packed in
     water or 1 (3 oz.) can tuna packed in spring water,
     drained and flaked
     Contents of the bag

Empty the contents of the bag into a large skillet. Stir in the water. Bring to a boil, stirring constantly. Add the other ingredients. Cover and return to a boil. Reduce heat and simmer for 20 to 30 minutes or until the rice is tender. (6 servings)

QUICK CHICKEN STIR FRY

Recipe for the bag:

1	tablespoon cornstarch
1	tablespoon instant potato flakes
1	packet of low sodium chicken flavored bouillon (about ½ tablespoon)
1	tablespoon dried celery flakes
1	teaspoon mild Indian curry powder
1	teaspoon dried chopped onions
½	teaspoon granulated white sugar
¼	teaspoon ground ginger
⅛	teaspoon white pepper

Mix all the ingredients and store in a plastic bag.

Recipe for completing:

1	lb. boned chicken breasts fillets, cut into ¼" pieces
1	(14 oz.) package frozen stir fry vegetables
1	(8 oz.) can sliced mushrooms, undrained
1	(6 oz.) package frozen snow pea pods
¾	cup water
4	tablespoons low sodium soy sauce
2	tablespoons olive oil
1	tablespoon cooking sherry (optional)

Contents of the bag

Heat the olive oil in wok or a skillet. Add the chicken and cook and stir until the chicken turns white in color. Stir in the mushrooms, stir fry vegetables, and the pea pods. Stir for 1 to 2 minutes. Add the contents of the bag to the water, in a separate bowl. Stir well. Add the sherry (if using) and the soy sauce to this mixture. Blend and then pour into the wok or skillet with the other ingredients. Cook and stir for 1 to 2 minutes or until thickened. Serve over hot cooked rice. (4 servings)

BAKED HERBED CHICKEN

Recipe for the bag:

⅓   cup instant potato flakes
⅓   cup biscuit mix
3   tablespoons Parmesan cheese
1½ teaspoons paprika
1   teaspoon dried parsley flakes
1   teaspoon dried cilantro leaves
1   teaspoon salt
½   teaspoon onion powder
½   teaspoon garlic powder
¼   teaspoon ground black pepper

Mix all the ingredients and seal in a plastic bag.

Recipe for completing:

2   lbs. chicken breast fillets, washed
1   tablespoon butter or margarine
Contents of the bag

Preheat the oven to 350 degrees. Melt the margarine in a 13" x 9" x 2" pan, in the oven. Coat the wet chicken with the contents of the bag. Place the coated chicken in the pan in a single layer. Bake, uncovered, for 30 minutes. Turn the chicken pieces and bake an additional 15 to 20 minutes or until the chicken is done. (6 to 8 servings)

"SKINNY" OVEN FRIED CHICKEN

Recipe for the bag:

1   cup biscuit mix (reduced-fat variety)
1   cup crushed corn flakes
1   teaspoon garlic powder
1   teaspoon celery salt
1   teaspoon paprika

Mix all the ingredients and seal in a plastic bag

Recipe for completing:

4   chicken breasts (8 pieces)
1   cup skimmed evaporated milk
Olive oil cooking spray
Contents of the bag

Wash the chicken breasts. Dip the chicken into the evaporated milk and then drop the chicken pieces into a large paper or plastic bag containing the bagged ingredients. Shake until the chicken is well coated. Repeat this process until you have coated all of the chicken. Line a pan with aluminum foil. Spray with the cooking spray. Place the chicken breasts on the foil in a single layer. Cover with another sheet of foil and bake at 350 degrees for 1 hour. Uncover and bake for 15 more minutes. (8 servings)

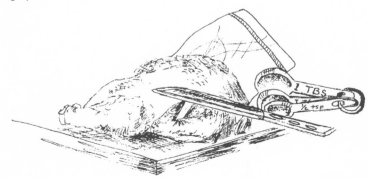

EASY CHICKEN AND RICE

Recipe for the bag:

1   cup long grain white rice
2   tablespoons chicken flavored bouillon granules
1   tablespoon dried chopped chives
½   teaspoon onion salt
⅛   teaspoon white pepper

Mix all the ingredients and store in a plastic bag.

Recipe for completing:

3   chicken breasts (6 pieces)
1   package dried onion-mushroom soup mix
2   cups water
Contents of the bag

Grease or spray a 13" x 9" x 2" baking dish or pan with shortening, margarine, butter, or olive oil cooking spray. Place the contents of the bag in the bottom of the dish or pan. Stir in the water and let stand a few minutes. Place the chicken pieces on top of the rice. Sprinkle the soup mix over the chicken. Cover and bake at 350 degrees for 1½ to 2 hours. (6 servings)

Side Dish

SIDE DISH

SCALLOPED TOMATOES

Recipe for the bag:

1   cup Italian bread crumbs (make your own by adding 1 tablespoon Italian seasoning to plain bread crumbs)
1   tablespoon dried minced onions
1   teaspoon granulated white sugar
½   teaspoon dried basil leaves
⅛   teaspoon ground red pepper or cayenne pepper

Combine all the ingredients and store in a plastic bag.

Recipe for completing:

1   (14½ oz.) can stewed tomatoes, undrained
2   tablespoons margarine or butter
Contents of the bag

Melt the butter or margarine in a one-quart casserole dish. Combine the contents of the bag with the tomatoes and melted margarine or butter. Pour into the casserole dish. Bake, covered, at 350 degrees for about 1 hour. (4 servings)

SIMPLE SQUASH CASSEROLE

Recipe for the bag:

2	tablespoons dried minced onions
1	tablespoon butter flavored granules
1	tablespoon cornstarch
1	tablespoon Italian style dry bread crumbs
½	teaspoon salt
¼	teaspoon black pepper
¼	teaspoon granulated white sugar

Combine all the ingredients and store in a plastic bag.

Recipe for completing:

1	lb. squash, sliced
1	egg, beaten
½	cup milk
½	cup grated cheddar cheese
	Contents of the bag

Cook the sliced squash in a small amount of water for about 20 minutes. Drain. Add all the remaining ingredients, including the contents of the bag, to the cooked squash. Place in an 8" square glass ovenproof dish. Bake, uncovered, in a 350 degree oven for 30 minutes. (6 servings)

STEAMED CABBAGE

Recipe for the bag:

2   tablespoons dried chopped onions
1   tablespoon beef flavored bouillon granules
1   tablespoon dried chopped chives
1   teaspoon garlic salt
½   teaspoon caraway seeds
½   teaspoon dried basil leaves

Mix all the ingredients and store in a plastic bag.

Recipe for completing:

1   medium cabbage, shredded
1   cup water
Contents of the bag

Bring the water to a boil in a medium saucepan. Stir in the contents of the bag. Add the cabbage. Cover and steam for 5 minutes. (6 servings)

INSTANT CORN AND CHEESE GRITS

Recipe for the bag:

1⅓   cup instant grits
1   tablespoon dried minced onions
1   tablespoon real bacon bits or pieces
1   tablespoon butter flavored granules
½   teaspoon salt
¼   teaspoon white pepper
⅛   teaspoon mustard powder

Combine all the ingredients and store in a plastic bag.

Recipe for completing:

2   cups water
⅓   cup shredded cheddar cheese
1   (8.5 oz.) can cream style corn
Contents of the bag

Combine the water and the cream style corn to equal about 2½ cups of liquid. Bring to a boil in a medium saucepan. Stir in the contents of the bag. Remove from heat and continue to stir until well blended. Fold in the cheese and serve hot. (6 servings)

CHILI TOMATO GRITS

Recipe for the bag:

1   cup quick grits (not instant)
1/4   cup real bacon pieces
1   tablespoon chicken flavored bouillon granules
1/4   teaspoon salt
1/8   teaspoon white pepper

Combine all the ingredients and store in a plastic bag.

Recipe for completing:

3 1/2 cups water
1   (10 oz.) can tomatoes and green chili peppers,
       undrained
1   cup shredded cheddar cheese
Contents of the bag

Bring the water to a boil in a medium saucepan. Stir in the tomatoes and chili peppers and the contents of the bag. Return to a boil. Reduce heat, cover, and simmer for about 20 minutes, stirring several times. Add the cheese, remove from heat and let stand until the cheese melts. Stir and serve. (6 servings)

POTATOES AU GRATIN

Recipe for the bag:

2   tablespoons all purpose flour
1   teaspoon dried chopped chives
1   teaspoon salt
½   teaspoon paprika
¼   teaspoon white pepper

Combine all the ingredients and store in a small plastic bag.

Recipe for completing:

6   medium potatoes
1   cup milk
1   cup grated cheddar cheese
2   tablespoons butter or margarine
Contents of the bag

Peel and slice the raw potatoes. Put into a medium saucepan and cover with the water. After the water begins to boil, cook for about 15 minutes. Drain and place in an 11" x 7" x 2" oven-proof dish or pan. Sprinkle contents of the bag over the potatoes, evenly. Combine the milk and butter or margarine and heat until butter or margarine melts. Pour over the potatoes. Bake at 350 degrees for about 15 minutes. Remove from the oven and sprinkle on the cheese. Return to the oven for 5 to 10 minutes or until the cheese melts. (6 to 8 servings)

PARMESAN POTATO BITES

Recipe for the bag:

1	cup self-rising flour
1	cup Parmesan cheese
1	teaspoon onion powder
1	teaspoon garlic powder
1	teaspoon dried parsley flakes, crushed
⅛	teaspoon white pepper
⅛	teaspoon salt

Combine all the ingredients and store in a plastic bag that is large enough to use for coating the potatoes.

Recipe for completing:

8	medium baking potatoes
1	stick butter or margarine
	Contents of the bag

Preheat the oven to 375 degrees. Melt the butter or margarine in a large broiling pan or heavy cookie sheet with sides. Peel the potatoes and cut into bite size pieces. Drop into cold water as you peel and cut, so that the potatoes will be crisp and do not become discolored. Lift the potatoes from the water and drop into the bag with the coating mix, a few pieces at the time, until all the potato bites are coated. Place in the pan with the melted butter or margarine in a single layer. Bake for 1 hour, turning several times for even browning. (8 servings)

GREAT GREEN PEAS FROM A CAN

Recipe for the bag:

1	tablespoon self-rising flour
1/4	teaspoon ground black pepper
1/4	teaspoon seasoned salt
1/4	teaspoon onion powder
1/8	teaspoon garlic powder

Combine all the ingredients and store in a plastic bag.

Recipe for completing:

1	(15 oz.) can small green peas or small green peas with onions and mushrooms
2	tablespoons butter or margarine
	Contents of the bag

Drain the peas but reserve the juice (about 3/4 cup). Set aside. Melt the butter or margarine over medium heat, being careful not to burn. When melted, stir in the contents of the bag. Mix thoroughly. Slowly add the reserved juice, a little at the time, continuing to sir as you pour. When finished, you should have a smooth sauce that has thickened somewhat. Add the peas and heat thoroughly. Do not boil. Serve hot. (4 to 6 servings)

GREEN BEANS ALMONDINE

Recipe for the bag:

Bag # 1

1	tablespoon dried chopped onions
1	tablespoon butter flavored granules
1	teaspoon chicken bouillon granules
¼	teaspoon dried minced garlic
⅛	teaspoon mild Indian curry powder
⅛	teaspoon salt
⅛	teaspoon ground black pepper

Combine all the ingredients and store in a plastic bag.

Bag # 2

2	tablespoons slivered almonds
1	tablespoon real bacon bits

Combine the ingredients and store in a plastic bag.

Recipe for completing:

1	(16 oz.) can whole green beans, drained
½	bean can water (about 1 cup)
	Contents of both bags

Rinse the drained green beans. Set aside. Combine the water and contents of bag # 1 in a medium saucepan. Bring to a boil. Stir in the green beans. Simmer until the beans are heated thoroughly. Transfer the beans to a serving dish, using a slotted spoon. Sprinkle the contents of bag # 2 over the beans, when ready to serve. (4 to 6 servings)

BAKED BARBECUED BEANS

Recipe for the bag:

2   tablespoons dried minced onions
1   tablespoon granulated brown sugar
1   teaspoon chili powder
1   teaspoon garlic powder
1   teaspoon mustard powder
½   teaspoon salt
¼   teaspoon ground black pepper

Combine all the ingredients and store in a plastic bag.

Recipe for completing:

2   (16 oz.) cans pork and beans, undrained
1   (16 oz.) can red kidney beans, drained
1   (15 oz.) can lima beans, drained
2   tablespoons tomato catsup
1   tablespoon Worcestershire sauce
1   tablespoon cider vinegar
3   strips of bacon
Contents of the bag

Combine all the ingredients and mix well. Place in a 13" x 9" x 2" ovenproof dish or pan. Lay the bacon slices across the top. Bake, uncovered, at 400 degrees for about 45 minutes. (8 servings)

LIMA BEAN CASSEROLE
Recipe for the bag:

Bag # 1

1   (16 oz.) bag large dry lima beans
1   (16 oz.) bag small dry lima beans
1   (16 oz.) bag green dry lima beans

Combine the beans and divide into four equal portions and store in 4 separate plastic bags (about 2 cups each).

Bag # 2

8   tablespoons granulated brown sugar
8   tablespoons dried chopped onions
8   teaspoons mustard powder
6   teaspoons salt
1   teaspoon ground black pepper

Combine all the ingredients and divide into 4 equal portions. Store in small plastic bags (about 5 tablespoons each).

Recipe for completing:

1   (10¾ oz.) can condensed tomato soup
1½ cup bean liquor
⅓   cup cider vinegar
1   tablespoon Worcestershire sauce
4 or 5 strips of bacon
Contents of both bags

Wash and sort the beans (Bag # 1). Cover with water and soak overnight. Drain. Add 2 quarts of fresh water. Cook for 1 hour. Drain, reserving 1½ cups of the bean liquor or juice. Empty the beans into a 13" x 9" x 2" casserole dish. Stir the contents of bag # 2 into the bean liquor. Add this mixture to the tomato soup, vinegar, and the Worcestershire sauce. Pour this mixture over the beans that you have placed into the casserole dish and stir well. Top with the bacon strips. Bake, uncovered, in a 450 degree oven for 45 minutes. (8 servings)

QUICK LIMA BEAN CASSEROLE

Recipe for the bag:

2   tablespoons granulated brown sugar
2   tablespoons dried chopped onions
2   tablespoons mustard powder
½   teaspoon salt
¼   teaspoon white pepper

Mix all the ingredients and store in a plastic bag.

Recipe for completing:

1   (15 oz.) can dried lima beans
1   (15 oz.) can fordhook lima beans
1   (15 oz.) can baby lima beans
1   (10¾ oz.) can condensed tomato soup
⅓   cup cider vinegar
1   tablespoon Worcestershire sauce
4 or 5 slices of bacon
Contents of the bag

Drain all the beans in a medium container (reserve 1½ cups of the combined liquid). Place the drained beans in a greased 13" x 9" x 2" casserole dish. Add the contents of the bag to the reserved bean liquid. Add the tomato soup, Worcestershire sauce and the vinegar. Pour this mixture over the beans and stir. Top with the bacon slices. Bake, uncovered, at 400 degrees for about 45 minutes. (8 servings)

CHILI TOMATO RICE

Recipe for the bag:

1	cup rice
1	tablespoon butter flavored granules
1	tablespoon dried celery flakes
1	tablespoon dried sweet bell pepper flakes
1	teaspoon dried minced garlic
1	teaspoon dried oregano leaves
1	teaspoon dried parsley flakes
1	teaspoon dried cilantro leaves
¼	teaspoon salt
¼	teaspoon paprika
⅛	teaspoon black pepper
⅛	teaspoon cayenne pepper

Combine all the ingredients and store in a plastic bag.

Recipe for completing:

1	(10 oz.) can tomatoes and green chili peppers, undrained
2	cups water
	Contents of the bag

Combine the tomatoes with chili peppers and the water in a medium saucepan. Bring to a boil. Stir in the contents of the bag. Return to a boil, then reduce heat, cover, and simmer for about 20 minutes or until rice is tender. (6 servings)

MICRO-BROWN RICE

Recipe for the bag:

1½ cups instant brown rice
1   tablespoon chicken flavored bouillon granules
1   tablespoon dried chopped onions
1   teaspoon dried basil leaves
1   teaspoon dried parsley leaves
⅛   teaspoon ground sage

Combine all the ingredients and store in a plastic bag.

Recipe for completing:

1¼ cups water
Contents of the bag

In a two-quart microwave safe casserole dish, combine the water and the contents of the bag. Cover and microwave on high for 8 minutes. Fluff with a fork and serve. (4 servings)

HERBED RICE

Recipe for the bag:

4   cups long grain white rice
4   tablespoons chicken flavored bouillon granules
2½ tablespoons dried parsley flakes
2   tablespoons dried chopped onions
1   tablespoon dried basil leaves
1   teaspoon ground thyme
1   teaspoon dried tarragon leaves
1   teaspoon garlic powder
¼   teaspoon onion powder
¼   teaspoon celery salt

Mix all the ingredients in a large container. Divide into 4 equal portions and seal in 4 separate plastic bags (about 1 cup plus 2 tablespoons per bag).

Recipe for completing:

2½ cups hot water
Contents of 1 bag

In a two-quart casserole dish, combine the contents of the bag with the water. Stir well. Preheat oven to 350 degrees. Cover and bake for 1 hour. Serve with sliced turkey or chicken breast. (4 to 6 servings)

SEASONED GARDEN RICE

Recipe for the bag:

1   cup long grain white rice
1   package dry savory herb with garlic soup mix
1   teaspoon chicken flavored bouillon granules
⅛   teaspoon ground black pepper

Mix all the ingredients and seal in a plastic bag.

Recipe for completing:

1   (15 oz.) can small early peas with pearl onions and
     mushrooms, undrained
2   cups hot water
Contents of the bag

Empty the contents of the bag into a two-quart casserole dish.
Stir in the water and the undrained peas with pearl onions and
mushrooms. Cover and bake for 1 hour at 350 degrees (162
calories and less than 1 gram of fat per serving). (6 servings)

SPANISH RICE

Recipe for the bag:

1   cup long grain white rice
1   tablespoon butter flavored granules
1   tablespoon dried sweet bell pepper flakes
1   tablespoon dried celery flakes
1   tablespoon dried chopped onions
1   teaspoon chili powder
1   teaspoon ground thyme
1   teaspoon paprika
½   teaspoon garlic powder
½   teaspoon onion powder
½   teaspoon salt
¼   teaspoon white pepper

Mix all the ingredients and seal in a plastic bag.

Recipe for completing:

1   (15 oz.) can stewed tomatoes, drained but reserve
     the juice
Contents of the bag

Add enough water to the reserved tomato juice to make two
cups of liquid. Empty into a medium saucepan. Bring the liquid
to a boil. Add the tomatoes and contents of the bag. Return to
a boil, stir, reduce heat, and simmer for 20 to 30 minutes or
until the rice is tender. (6 servings)

RED RICE

Recipe for the bag:

1	cup long grain white rice
1	tablespoon dried sweet bell pepper flakes
1	tablespoon dried chopped onions
1	teaspoon dried cilantro leaves
1	teaspoon dried oregano leaves
½	teaspoon cumin
½	teaspoon dried minced garlic

Mix all the ingredients and store in a plastic bag.

Recipe for completing:

1	cup water
1	(15 oz.) can chunky Mexican tomato sauce
	Contents of the bag

Combine the water and the chunky Mexican tomato sauce in a medium saucepan. Bring to a boil. Stir in the contents of the bag. Reduce the heat and simmer for 30 minutes, until the rice is tender and the liquid is absorbed. Serve with a Mexican meal. (Serves 8)

BROWN RICE

Recipe for the bag:

1   cup long grain white rice
1   package dried onion soup mix
1   tablespoon butter flavored granules
1   teaspoon beef flavored bouillon granules

Mix all the ingredients and store in a plastic bag.

Recipe for completing:

1   (4 oz.) can sliced mushrooms, undrained
2½ cups hot water
Contents of the bag

In a two-quart casserole dish, combine the contents of the bag with the hot water. Stir in the mushrooms. Preheat oven to 350 degrees. Cover and bake for 1 hour. (6 servings)

TACO SALAD

Recipe for the bag:

1	tablespoon instant potato flakes
1	tablespoon cornstarch
1½	teaspoons ground cumin
1½	teaspoons chili powder
1½	teaspoons onion powder
1	teaspoon paprika
1	teaspoon garlic powder
1	teaspoon salt

Mix all the ingredients and store in a plastic bag.

Recipe for completing:

1	lb. ground beef
1	(15 oz.) can kidney beans, drained
1	(6 oz.) can tomato paste
¾	cup water
	Contents of the bag

Brown the ground beef. Drain well. Stir in the contents of the bag. Add the other ingredients. Bring to a boil. Reduce heat and simmer for 15 minutes, stirring occasionally. Serve over lettuce and corn chips. Top with sliced ripe olives, shredded cheddar cheese, chopped tomatoes, and chopped onions. You may also add sour cream and guacamole or salsa to this salad. (4 to 6 servings)

BASIC BEAN SALAD

Recipe for the bag:

1	tablespoon butter flavored granules
10	packets sugar substitute or ¾ cup granulated white sugar
½	teaspoon mustard powder
½	teaspoon dried tarragon leaves
½	teaspoon dried basil leaves
¼	teaspoon garlic powder
¼	teaspoon white pepper

Mix all the ingredients and store in a plastic bag.

Recipe for completing:

½	cup cider vinegar
¼	cup hot tap water
1	tablespoon olive oil
1	(14½ oz.) can green beans, drained and rinsed
1	(14½ oz.) can yellow wax beans, drained and rinsed
1	(14½ oz.) can red kidney beans, drained and rinsed
1	small onion, chopped
1	small green pepper, seeded and chopped
1	(4 oz.) jar chopped red pimiento, drained
	Contents of the bag

Place the drained and rinsed beans in a large container. Add the chopped onion, bell pepper, and the pimiento. Add the water to the contents of the bag, in a separate bowl. Stir well. Add the vinegar and the oil to this mixture. Pour over the vegetables. Cover and marinate overnight. Serve chilled. (8 servings)

NIFTY FIFTIES NOODLE CASSEROLE

Recipe for the bag:

1   tablespoon butter flavored granules
1   tablespoon dried chopped chives
1   tablespoon dried parsley flakes
1   teaspoon dried basil leaves
½   teaspoon garlic powder
¼   teaspoon salt
⅛   teaspoon ground black pepper
⅛   teaspoon dried oregano leaves

Combine all the ingredients and store in a plastic bag.

Recipe for completing:

1   (10 oz.) package no yolk egg noodles
1   (16 oz.) can small English peas, drained
¾   cup grated Parmesan cheese
½   cup sour cream
½   cup ricotta cheese or small curd cottage cheese
2   tablespoons milk
Contents of the bag

Cook the noodles less than the package suggests. Drain and rinse the noodles. Combine the ricotta or cottage cheese, the sour cream, and the milk. Stir in the contents of the bag, mixing well. Fold in the noodles and the peas. Empty mixture into an 8" square ovenproof dish or foil pan. Bake for about 10 minutes at 375 degrees. Remove from the oven. Sprinkle on the Parmesan cheese. Return to the oven for an additional 5 minutes. Serve hot. (6 servings)

CRISPY OVEN-BAKED VEGGIES

Recipe for the bag:

½   cup dried instant potato flakes
¼   cup grated Parmesan cheese (the canned type)
½   teaspoon garlic powder
¼   teaspoon dried basil leaves, crushed
¼   teaspoon dried parsley flakes, crushed

Combine and store in a large resealable plastic bag and keep refrigerated, if not using immediately, because of the cheese.

Recipe for completing:

2 to 3 cups assorted cut up vegetables such as
     broccoli, cauliflower, carrots, yellow squash, zucchini
     squash, or mushrooms
½   stick of butter or margarine
1   egg, beaten
Contents of the bag

Heat the oven to 400 degrees. Melt the butter or margarine in a heavy cookie sheet with sides or a roasting pan. Remove pan from the oven when the butter or margarine has melted. Dip the vegetables into the beaten egg, coating each piece. Drop egg coated vegetables into the bag with the coating mix, a few pieces at the time. Shake to cover well.
Remove pieces from the bag and place on the sheet or pan with the melted butter or margarine. Repeat the process until all the veggies are coated. Bake for 10 minutes. Turn the vegetables and cook for another 10 minutes. Remove with a spatula and serve hot. (2 to 3 servings)

SOUTHERN STEWED CORN

Recipe for the bag:

1   tablespoon all purpose flour
1   teaspoon granulated white sugar
½   teaspoon salt
¼   teaspoon ground black pepper

Mix all the ingredients and store in a plastic bag.

Recipe for completing:

2   cups fresh corn (cut from the cob)
¾   cup water
¼   cup milk
2   tablespoons butter or margarine
1   tablespoon corn oil
Contents of the bag

Put the corn in a medium saucepan. Add water, butter or margarine and oil. Cook over medium heat for about 10 minutes. Add the milk, a little at the time, to the contents of the bag. Make a paste, then gradually add the remainder of the milk. This eliminates lumps. Stir this mixture into the corn, stirring as it thickens. Reduce the heat and simmer for 5 minutes. Check and stir often or the corn will stick to the bottom of the pan. (Serves 4)

Sweets

SWEETS

FRESH STRAWBERRY PIE

Recipe for the bag:

1   cup granulated white sugar
3½ tablespoons cornstarch
3   tablespoons strawberry gelatin
1   teaspoon vanilla powder

Combine all the ingredients and store in a plastic bag.

Recipe for completing:

4   cups fresh strawberries, sliced
1   cup boiling water
1   (10") pie shell (baked according to package
    directions)
Contents of the bag

Combine the contents of the bag with the boiling water in a medium saucepan. Cook and stir the mixture, after it comes to a boil, for about 5 minutes. The mixture should look clear or transparent. Cool. Place the sliced strawberries in the baked and cooled pie shell. Pour the cooled mix over the strawberries. Refrigerate for 3 or 4 hours. Slice and serve. You may add your favorite whipped topping. (Serves 8 to 10)

BROWNIES IN A BAG

Recipe for the bag:

1   cup white granulated sugar
⅔ cup cocoa
½ cup self-rising flour
½ cup pecan pieces
1   teaspoon vanilla powder

Combine all the ingredients and store in a plastic bag.

Recipe for completing:

½ cup cooking oil
2   eggs, beaten
Contents of the bag

Combine the eggs and the oil. Gradually stir in the contents of the bag until well blended. Pour the batter into a well-greased 9" square pan. Bake in a 350 degree oven for 25 to 30 minutes. Brownies will pull away from the side of the pan, when done. Cut into 12 squares and serve. (Yield 12 squares)

BUTTERSCOTCH CHIP PIE

Recipe for the bag:

1   cup pecan pieces
1   cup butterscotch pieces
½   cup self-rising flour
½   cup granulated white sugar
½   cup granulated brown sugar
1   teaspoon vanilla powder

Mix all the ingredients and store in a plastic bag.

Recipe for the bag:

1   unbaked (9") pie crust
1   stick butter or margarine, melted
2   large eggs, beaten
Contents of the bag

Combine the beaten eggs with the melted margarine or butter.
Stir in the contents of the bag. Pour into the unbaked pie crust.
Bake at 350 degrees for 30 minutes. Serve with whipped
cream.   (6 to 8 servings)

PECAN COOKIES

Recipe for the bag:

1½ cups chopped pecans
½   cup granulated white sugar
½   cup granulated brown sugar
4   tablespoons self-rising flour
1   tablespoon vanilla powder

Mix all the ingredients and store in a plastic bag.

Recipe for completing:

1   stick butter or margarine, melted
1   egg, beaten
Contents of the bag

Mix together the butter or margarine and the egg. Stir in the contents of the bag. Line a cookie sheet with aluminum foil. Spray with cooking oil. Drop the batter onto the foil in half teaspoon portions. Bake at 325 degrees for about 10 minutes. Cool on a wire rack after removing from the foil lined pan. You may roll in powdered sugar, if desired.
(Yield 2 dozen cookies)

GOOD FOR YOU COOKIES

Recipe for the bag:

2   cups quick cooking oats
½   cup raisins
½   cup pecan pieces
½   cup chocolate chips

Mix all the ingredients and store in a plastic bag.

Recipe for completing:

⅓   cup vegetable oil
3   medium ripe bananas
¼   cup peanut butter
Contents of the bag

Mash the bananas. Stir in the peanut butter. Add the oil and contents of the bag. Let stand for 30 minutes. Drop by table-spoons onto non-greased cookie sheets. Bake at 300 degrees for 30 minutes. (2 dozen cookies)

CHAMELEON COOKIES

Recipe for the bag:

1   cup instant potato flakes
1   cup white granulated sugar
1   (5.5 oz.) package buttermilk biscuit mix
1   (3.4 oz.) package instant pudding and pie mix*
1   teaspoon vanilla powder

*The flavor of the cookie is determined by the flavor of the pudding and pie mix, so you may change as often as you wish. You may choose lemon pudding and have lemon cookies, chocolate pudding and have chocolate cookies, pistachio pudding for pistachio cookies, coconut pudding for coconut cookies, etc.

Combine all the ingredients and store in a plastic bag.

Recipe for completing:

1   stick melted butter or margarine
1   egg, beaten
Contents of the bag

Combine all the ingredients and mix by hand. Let stand for 15 minutes. Roll into small balls and place on a non-greased cookie sheet, about 2" apart. Preheat oven to 350 degrees. Bake until lightly browned, about 8 to 10 minutes. (Yields 4½ dozen cookies)

QUICK PEACH DESSERT

Recipe for the bag:

1   cup self-rising flour
1   cup white granulated sugar
1   teaspoon vanilla powder
1   teaspoon ground cinnamon

Combine all the ingredients and store in a plastic bag.

Recipe for completing:

1   (16 oz.) can sliced peaches
1   stick butter or margarine
Contents of the bag

Drain the peaches, reserving 2/3 cup of the juice. In a medium bowl, combine the peach juice and the contents of the bag. Mix well. Melt the margarine in an 8" square pan or ovenproof dish. Pour the batter over the melted margarine. Do not stir. Arrange the drained peaches over the batter. Bake at 350 degrees for 45 minutes or until browned. Serve hot, with vanilla ice cream or whipped topping. (4 to 6 servings)

BANANA PUDDING CUPS

Recipe for the bag:

1   package dry whipped topping mix
1   (3.4 oz.) package instant banana cream pudding
      and pie mix
1   teaspoon vanilla powder

Mix all the ingredients and store in a plastic bag.

Recipe for completing:

1½ cups milk
2   medium bananas
12 vanilla wafers
Contents of the bag
4   (9 oz.) ultra clear plastic cups

Mix the contents of the bag with the milk. Beat 3 or 4 minutes
or until the mixture begins to thicken. Crumble 3 vanilla wafers
into the bottom of each cup. Top with 2 tablespoons of pudding
mix, 5 banana slices, another 2 tablespoons of mix, another 5
banana slices and finish with 2 more tablespoons of pudding
mix. Garnish the parfait' with a banana slice, if desired. Refrigerate. (4 servings)

RED HOT APPLES

Recipe for the bag:

½ cup granulated white sugar
½ cup granulated brown sugar
½ cup red hot cinnamon candies
1 tablespoon butter flavored granules
1 tablespoon cornstarch

Mix all the ingredients and store in a plastic bag.

Recipe for completing:

4 cups cored, peeled, and sliced apples
1 cup water
Contents of the bag

Toss the sliced apples with the contents of the bag. Stir in the water. Place in a greased 11" x 7" x 1½" casserole dish. Bake, covered, at 350 degrees for 1   hour. Stir well before serving. (4 to 6 servings)

CARMEL APPLE COBBLER

Recipe for the bag:

½   cup pecan pieces
½   cup butterscotch pieces
¼   cup granulated brown sugar
2   tablespoons self-rising flour
½   teaspoon apple pie spice
½   teaspoon ground cinnamon

Combine all the ingredients and store in a plastic bag.

Recipe for completing:

1   cup orange juice
1   (21 oz.) can apple pie filling
1   regular 9" frozen pie crust
Contents of the bag

Stir the contents of the bag into the juice. Combine this mixture with the pie filling. Pour into an 11" x 7" x 1½" casserole dish. Crumble the frozen piecrust over the top. Preheat oven to 350 degrees. Bake for 45 minutes. Top the hot cobbler with a scoop of vanilla ice cream. (8 servings)

OVEN GLAZED YAMS

Recipe for the bag:

½   cup granulated white sugar
½   cup granulated brown sugar
1   tablespoon cornstarch
1   tablespoon dried orange peel
1   teaspoon ground nutmeg
1   teaspoon vanilla powder
1   teaspoon pumpkin pie spice

Mix all the ingredients and store in a plastic bag.

Recipe for completing:

1   (29 oz.) can yams or sweet potatoes
1   cup pineapple juice
½   stick butter or margarine
Contents of the bag

Drain the yams or sweet potatoes. Slice and place in a baking dish. Melt the margarine or butter. Stir into the melted butter or margarine the juice and the contents of the bag. Place in a saucepan and bring to a boil over medium heat. Stir continuously until thickened. Pour this mixture over the yams or sweet potatoes. Preheat oven to 350 degrees and bake for 15 to 20 minutes or until completely heated. (4 to 6 servings)

MOLASSES SPICE CAKE

Recipe for the bag:

2 cups self-rising flour
1 cup granulated brown sugar
1 teaspoon ground cinnamon
1 teaspoon ground ginger
1 teaspoon vanilla powder
½ teaspoon ground cloves

Combine all the ingredients and store in a plastic bag.

Recipe for completing:

1½ sticks butter or margarine, melted
¼   cup molasses
1   egg, beaten
Contents of the bag

Combine the first three ingredients in a bowl. Stir in the contents of the bag. Mix well. Pour into an 8" square greased cake pan. Bake at 350 degrees for 30 minutes. Sprinkle with powdered sugar. (Makes 9 squares)

CORN FLAKE PEANUT MORSELS

Recipe for the bag:

1	cup self-rising flour
1	cup corn flake crumbs
1/3	cup brown sugar, packed
1/3	cup peanut butter morsels
1/4	cup white granulated sugar
1	teaspoon dried lemon peel
1	teaspoon dried orange peel
1	teaspoon ground cinnamon
1	teaspoon vanilla powder

Mix all the ingredients and store in a plastic bag.

Recipe for completing:

1/3	cup vegetable oil
1	egg, beaten
	Contents of the bag

Mix together the oil, egg, and the contents of the bag. Form into small balls and place on a non-greased cookie sheet. Bake at 375 degrees for 8 to 10 minutes, until lightly browned. Cool on a wire rack. When completely cooled, store in an airtight container.
(Yields 2 dozen cookies)

ORANGE RUM BALLS

Recipe for the bag:

2	cups vanilla wafer crumbs
1	cup powdered sugar
1	cup pecan pieces
¼	cup cocoa
1	teaspoon ground cinnamon
1	teaspoon dried orange peel

Mix all the ingredients and store in a plastic bag.

Recipe for completing:

¼	cup orange juice
¼	cup rum
2 tablespoons corn syrup
Contents of the bag

Mix together the juice, rum, and syrup. Stir in the contents of the bag. Add more crumbs if the dough is not stiff enough and add more juice if the dough is too stiff. Roll the balls in additional powdered sugar and store in an airtight container. (The number depends on the size of the balls)

CAROLINA CLUSTERS

Recipe for the bag:

Bag # 1

2 cups white granulated sugar
3 tablespoons cocoa
1 teaspoon vanilla powder

Bag # 2

3 cups quick cooking oats
1¾ cups or 1 (10 oz.) package peanut butter chips
1 cup chopped walnuts

Combine ingredients in 2 separate plastic bags. Label as bag # 1 and bag # 2.

Recipe for completing:

1 stick butter or margarine
½ cup milk
Contents of both bags

Combine the margarine or butter and the milk in a medium saucepan. Heat until the margarine or butter is melted. Stir in the contents of bag # 1. Stirring continuously, bring to a boil and boil for 2 minutes. Remove from the heat and stir in the contents of bag # 2. Mix well. Drop by tablespoons onto wax paper. Cool and store in an airtight container. (Yields about 40 cookies)

VANILLA WAFER FUDGE FINGERS

Recipe for the bag:

2   cups vanilla wafer crumbs* crushed in a food processor or blender (may use the reduced-fat variety)
2   cups chopped pecans
3/4 cup cocoa
1   teaspoon vanilla powder
1   teaspoon ground cinnamon
1/8 teaspoon salt
*32 vanilla wafers = 1 cup crumbs

Combine all the ingredients and store in a plastic bag.

Recipe for completing:

1   (14 oz.) can sweetened condensed milk (may use fat-free milk)
1/2 stick butter or margarine, melted
Contents of the bag
Powdered sugar (about 1 cup)

Melt the butter or margarine in a 13" x 9" x 2" baking dish or pan. With a pastry brush, grease the entire dish or pan including the sides. In another bowl combine the melted margarine, poured from the dish or pan, milk and the contents of the bag. Mixture will be thick and sticky. Pat the mixture into the dish or pan. Chill in the refrigerator overnight. Cut into 12 squares, then cut each square into 3 fingers. Roll the fingers in the extra powdered sugar. Store in the refrigerator. Will keep 2 weeks. (Yields 36 fingers)

SWEET POTATO PIE

Recipe for the bag:

½   cup granulated white sugar
½   cup biscuit mix
2   teaspoons vanilla powder
1   teaspoon ground cinnamon
1   teaspoon ground nutmeg
½   teaspoon salt
½   teaspoon ground mace

Combine all the ingredients and store in a plastic bag.

Recipe for completing:

1   (29 oz.) can sweet potatoes, drained and mashed
2   eggs, beaten
1   (5 oz.) can evaporated milk plus enough water to
     make 1   cup liquid
2   tablespoons butter or margarine, melted
Contents of the bag

Preheat the oven to 350 degrees. Melt the butter or margarine in a 10" glass pie plate. Coat the plate with the melted butter or margarine. Then, add the melted butter or margarine with the remaining ingredients in a blender. Blend until smooth. Pour into the already greased pie plate. Bake for 50 to 55 minutes or until done. Cut and serve. May garnish with whipped cream or topping. (8 to 10 servings)

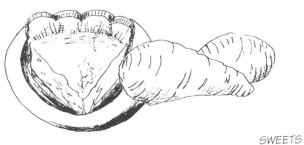

FRIED APPLES

Recipe for the bag:

½   cup raisins
¼   cup granulated white sugar
¼   cup granulated brown sugar
1   tablespoon cornstarch
1   teaspoon ground cinnamon
1   teaspoon vanilla powder
¼   teaspoon ground nutmeg
¼   teaspoon ground allspice
¼   teaspoon ground cloves

Combine all the ingredients and store in a plastic bag.

Recipe for completing:

8   apples, cored, peeled and sliced (about 6 cups
    sliced apples)
2   tablespoons butter or margarine
1   cup water
Contents of the bag

Melt the butter or margarine in a heavy iron skillet. Mix the
apples with the contents of the bag. Add the water. Place the
apple mixture in the skillet with the melted butter or margarine.
Cook slowly over medium heat, turning often to prevent sticking,
until mixture is thickened and the apples are cooked. Cook
about 15 minutes covered and 15 minutes uncovered. (Yield 6
servings)

QUICK APPLE COBBLER

Recipe for the bag:

Bag # 1
½   cup granulated white sugar
1   teaspoon ground cinnamon
1   teaspoon ground apple pie spice

Bag # 2
1½ cups biscuit mix (may use lower fat variety)
½   cup granulated brown sugar
½   cup granulated white sugar
1   teaspoon vanilla powder

Combine the ingredients separately and store in 2 plastic bags. Label as Bag # 1 and Bag # 2.

Recipe for completing:

6   cups apples, cored, peeled and sliced
1   egg, beaten
1   stick margarine or butter
Contents of both bags

Combine the sliced apples with the contents of bag # 1. Place in a greased 13" x 9" x 2" ovenproof casserole dish or pan. Mix the egg with the contents of bag # 2. Spread crumb mixture over the apples. Melt the butter or margarine and pour over the top. Bake at 350 degrees for about 45 minutes. Spoon into dishes. Add a scoop of vanilla ice cream to the hot cobbler, if desired. (6 to 8 servings)

CHEWY CHOCOLATE COCONUT COOKIES

Recipe for the bag:

1	cup self-rising flour
1	cup semi-sweet chocolate morsels
⅓	cup granulated brown sugar
⅓	cup granulated white sugar
½	cup dry roasted lightly salted peanuts, chopped
½	cup flaked coconut
½	cup raisins
1	teaspoon vanilla powder

Combine all the ingredients and store in a reuseable plastic bag.

Recipe for completing:

1	stick butter or margarine, melted
1	egg, beaten
	Contents of the bag

Combine the melted butter or margarine and the beaten egg. Gradually add the contents of the bag, blending well. Drop by heaping teaspoon onto ungreased baking sheets. Preheat oven to 375 degrees. Bake for 10 minutes. Let cool in pan for 5 minutes. Remove cookies to wire rack until cooled completely. Store in covered container. (Makes about 30 cookies)

Et Cetera

ET CETERA

BAG YOUR OWN SOUP

Recipe for the bag:

1	cup non-fat instant dry milk
6	tablespoons cornstarch
2	tablespoons chicken flavored bouillon granules
1	tablespoon dried chopped onions
1	tablespoon instant potato flakes
1	tablespoon butter flavored granules
½	teaspoon dried basil leaves
½	teaspoon ground thyme

Mix all the ingredients and store in a plastic bag.

Recipe for completing:

1	cup water
5	tablespoons mix from the bag

Combine the mix with the water. Stir to moisten. Heat, covered, in a microwave oven for 1 minute at 100 % power. Heat until thickened. This equals 1 can of condensed soup and can be used in casseroles or soups as a thickening agent.

BAG YOUR OWN SALT SUBSTITUTE

Recipe for the bag:

6   tablespoons onion powder
3   tablespoons ground sage
3   tablespoons paprika
2   tablespoons mustard powder
1   tablespoon garlic powder
2   teaspoons white pepper
2   teaspoons ground oregano
1   teaspoon chili powder

Mix all the ingredients and store in a plastic bag.

Recipe for completing:

Use on a salt restricted diet to season food instead of using salt. Use according to your own individual taste. You may wish to use in your salt shaker instead of salt.

BAG YOUR OWN BARBECUE SAUCE

Recipe for the bag:

3	tablespoons granulated brown sugar
1	tablespoon chili powder
1	tablespoon garlic powder
1	tablespoon paprika
1	teaspoon mustard powder
1	teaspoon lemon pepper
1	teaspoon onion powder
1/8	teaspoon dried lemon peel
1/8	teaspoon ground red pepper

Mix all the ingredients and store in a plastic bag.

Recipe for completing:

Sprinkle over chicken or other meats before baking or grilling instead of bottled barbecue sauce.

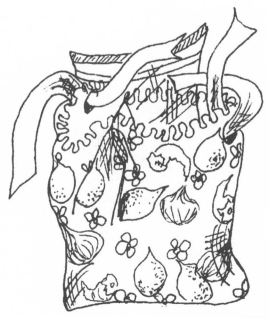

BAG YOUR OWN TACO SEASONING

Recipe for the bag:

3   tablespoons onion powder
3   tablespoons chili powder
3   tablespoons cornstarch
1½ tablespoons beef flavored bouillon granules
1   tablespoon dried oregano leaves
2   teaspoons ground cumin
1   teaspoon dried cilantro leaves
1   teaspoon paprika
1   teaspoon garlic powder
⅛   teaspoon salt
⅛   teaspoon white pepper
⅛   teaspoon ground cayenne pepper

Mix all the ingredients and store in a plastic bag.

Recipe for completing:

Remove from the bag as needed. Three tablespoons of mix is equal to 1¼ oz. of pre-packaged taco seasoning mix. (Makes enough to equal 4 packages)

GRAVY IN A BAG

Recipe for the bag:

1   tablespoon bouillon granules (beef flavored for beef gravy and chicken flavored for chicken gravy)
1   tablespoon dried chopped onions (optional)
⅓   cup self-rising flour
½   teaspoon sage or paprika*
¼   teaspoon celery salt
⅛   teaspoon white pepper
*Use paprika when making beef gravy instead of sage

Mix all the ingredients and store in a plastic bag.

Recipe for completing:

3   tablespoons butter or margarine
2   cups milk or 1 cup milk and 1 cup water
Contents of the bag

Melt the margarine or butter in a small skillet or saucepan. Stir in the contents of the bag and brown. Gradually add the milk or the milk and water. Stir constantly until the mixture is smooth and thickened. (Makes about 2 cups gravy)

SALAD ENHANCER

Recipe for the bag:

2   tablespoons small croutons or large crushed croutons
2   tablespoons imitation bacon bits
2   tablespoons grated Parmesan cheese
1   tablespoon sesame seeds
1   tablespoon chopped peanuts

Mix all the ingredients and store in a plastic bag.

Recipe for completing:

Use to enhance a tossed green salad. Pour oil and vinegar or a salad dressing of your choice over the salad. Sprinkle 1 table-spoon of the mix on top of the dressing. (Makes about 8 servings)

RANCH STYLE SALAD DRESSING

Recipe for the bag:

2   packages sugar substitute or 1 tablespoon sugar
2   tablespoons dry non-fat milk
1   teaspoon dried parsley flakes
1   teaspoon dried chopped chives
½   teaspoon garlic powder
½   teaspoon celery salt
½   teaspoon dill weed
⅛   teaspoon mustard powder
⅛   teaspoon white pepper

Mix all the ingredients and store in a plastic bag.

Recipe for completing:

¼   cup mayonnaise (may use fat free or reduced fat
     mayonnaise)
¼   cup rice vinegar
¼   cup salad oil
Contents of the bag

Stir the contents of the bag into the mayonnaise. Slowly add
the vinegar and oil. If mixture is too thick, add a little milk or
lemon juice. Keep refrigerated. May be used as a salad dressing
or as a dip for raw vegetables. (Makes about 1 cup of dressing)

POPPY SEED DRESSING
(LOW CALORIE AND FAT FREE)

Recipe for the bag:

6	packets sugar substitute
1	heaping teaspoon poppy seeds
1	teaspoon mustard powder
¼	teaspoon dried dill weed
¼	teaspoon dried parsley flakes
¼	teaspoon onion powder
¼	teaspoon garlic powder

Combine all the ingredients and store in a plastic bag.

Recipe for completing:

½	cup rice vinegar
6	tablespoons non-fat mayonnaise
2	tablespoons non-fat plain yogurt
1	teaspoon lemon juice
	Contents of the bag

Put all the ingredients in a blender. Blend until smooth. Put into a jar with a lid. Keep refrigerated. (Makes about 1½ cups) 3½ calories and 0 fat per tablespoon.

BAG YOUR OWN SEASONED CROUTONS

Recipe for the bag:

1   teaspoon dried parsley flakes
1   teaspoon dried basil leaves
1   teaspoon dried oregano leaves
1   teaspoon garlic powder
1   teaspoon onion powder

Combine all the ingredients and store in a plastic bag.

Recipe for completing:

4   cups bread cubes
3   tablespoons butter or margarine, melted
Contents of the bag

Freeze the bread slices. (Use 2 or 3 days old bread) On a cutting board, stack 3 slices of bread. With a bread knife, make cubes to equal 4 cups. Mix the contents of the bag with the melted margarine or butter. Pour over the bread cubes. Make sure that all of the bread is coated. Place in a jelly roll pan or cookie sheet with sides. Bake at 300 degrees for 30 to 45 minutes, stirring occasionally. Cool and store in an airtight container in the refrigerator or freeze until ready to use. (Yields 4 cups croutons)

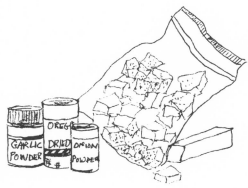

BAG YOUR OWN SEASONED BREAD CRUMBS

Recipe for the bag:

1	tablespoon dried basil leaves
1	tablespoon dried parsley flakes
1	tablespoon dried cilantro flakes
1	tablespoon dried green onions or chopped chives
1	teaspoon paprika
1	teaspoon ground sage
1	teaspoon garlic powder
1	teaspoon ground oregano

Combine all the ingredients and store in a plastic bag.

Recipe for completing:

3   cups bread crumbs
Contents of the bag

You may use any left over bread, such as hamburger buns, hot dog rolls, sliced bread, biscuits, etc. Crumb bread in a blender or food processor, a few pieces at the time. Mix the contents of the bag with the crumbs. Spread on a cookie sheet to dry. Store in an airtight container. Keep refrigerated or frozen until ready to use.

BAYOU BLEND

Recipe for the bag:

1	tablespoon chili powder
1	tablespoon paprika
1	tablespoon onion powder
1	tablespoon garlic powder
1	teaspoon ground cayenne pepper
1	teaspoon ground thyme
1	teaspoon ground oregano
1	teaspoon ground gumbo file'
1	teaspoon dehydrated minced red and green peppers
1	teaspoon celery salt

Combine all the ingredients and store in a plastic bag.

Recipe for completing:

Use in desired amounts for soups, stews, gumbo, or other low country recipes.

KITCHEN BOUQUET BAGS

Recipe for the bag:

1   teaspoon dried sage leaves
1   teaspoon dried thyme leaves
1   teaspoon dried marjoram leaves
1   teaspoon dried oregano leaves
1   dried bay leaf

Cut a piece of cheesecloth, doubled, into a 6" x 6" square. Put the herb leaves in the middle of the square. Draw up the corners to the middle. Secure with a clean cotton string. Store the bouquet bags in a large plastic bag. If you grow and dry your own herbs, use them.

Recipe for completing:

1   bouquet bag

Drop one bouquet bag into canned soups, stews, or broth for a special added flavor. Prepare canned items as you usually do. Remove the bag when ready to serve. Discard bag after using.

BOIL-A-SMELL BAGS
(SMELLS LIKE GRANDMA'S KITCHEN)

Recipe for the bag:

1   cinnamon stick (broken into small pieces)
1   teaspoon pickling spice
1   teaspoon whole cloves
½   teaspoon whole allspice
1   dried bay leaf

Cut a piece of doubled cheesecloth into a 6" x 6" squares. Put the spices in the middle of one square. Draw the corners together and hold tightly. Tie a clean cotton string around the middle to secure.

Recipe for completing:

2   cups water
1   boiling bag

Drop a bag into a small container with the water. Bring to a boil. Reduce heat and simmer for a wonderful fragrance in your kitchen. Check water often so that the pot will not boil dry. Add water as needed. Discard bag and water after using. (Use for fragrance only)

HOT DOG CHILI

Recipe for the bag:

1	teaspoon chili powder
½	teaspoon garlic powder
½	teaspoon onion powder
½	teaspoon cornstarch
¼	teaspoon paprika
¼	teaspoon ground black pepper
¼	teaspoon salt

Combine all the ingredients and store in a plastic bag.

Recipe for completing:

½	lb. ground beef
2	tablespoons water
1	tablespoon tomato catsup
	Contents of the bag

Brown the ground beef in a small skillet. Stir in the contents of the bag. Add the catsup and water. Stir until mixture begins to thicken. Keep warm and serve on hot dogs.
(Makes enough for 8 hot dogs)

CINNAMON SUGAR

Recipe for the bag:

½   cup granulated white sugar
¼   cup granulated brown sugar
1   teaspoon ground cinnamon
½   teaspoon vanilla powder

Combine all the ingredients and store in a plastic bag.

Recipe for completing:

Transfer, amount needed, to a shaker (glass or plastic container)
Shake on to flavor waffles, oatmeal, pancakes, French toast or buttered toast. Easy to make and adds a wonderful flavor.

For buttered cinnamon toast, spread a layer of softened butter or margarine on a slice of bread. Sprinkle on the cinnamon sugar according to taste. Pop under the broiler of your oven for a few minutes. Watch carefully. Do not let it burn. Your family will love it!

BAG YOUR OWN CITRUS PEEL

Recipe for the bag:

Collect citrus peelings from oranges, grapefruits, tangerines, lemons, and limes. Remove as much of the white membrane as you can. Place the peelings on a paper plate and let dry at room temperature for 5 or 6 days. Break into small pieces with your hands or use your kitchen shears. Peelings should break easily when dried. Do not use plastic or foam plates when drying.

Recipe for completing:

Use the dried peelings for seasoning tea, cider, wine, or for a boiling sachet. Use a cheesecloth square tied with a cotton string to hold your peelings when adding to hot liquid. When using as a potpourri, place in an open dish or basket. Do not confuse this type of peel with the fine dried lemon and orange peel used in baking.

SEASONING GUIDE

Beef-chili powder, rosemary, garlic, dill, paprika, curry powder, garlic, pepper

Beverages-all spice, cinnamon, cloves, lemon peel, orange peel, vanilla powder

Breads-Rolls-caraway seeds, poppy seeds, garlic, onion, pumpkin pie spice

Cakes-Cookies-allspice, cinnamon, ginger, mace, nutmeg, lemon peel, orange peel, poppy seed, vanilla powder

Chicken-Turkey-chili powder, coriander, cumin, curry powder, garlic, marjoram, paprika, pepper, poultry seasoning, sage

Dips-Spreads-chives, dill, chili powder, fennel, mustard powder, parsley, poppy seed

Eggs-marjoram, onion, chives, mustard powder, curry powder, parsley, black or white pepper, tarragon, turmeric

Fish-Seafood-basil, bay leaf, cayenne pepper, coriander, curry powder, fennel, rosemary, seafood seasoning, thyme

Fruit-apple pie spice, cinnamon, cloves, ginger, mace, vanilla powder, pumpkin pie spice

Lamb-curry powder, paprika, rosemary, thyme, sage, ginger, mustard seed

Marinades-bay leaf, garlic, Italian seasoning, parsley, rosemary

Pickles-cinnamon, cloves, whole allspice, dill, fennel, mustard powder

Pies-apple pie spice, cinnamon, cloves, mace, ginger, pumpkin pie spice

Pork-caraway seed, coriander, cloves, garlic, marjoram, paprika

Sauces-Dressings-allspice, apple pie spice, bay leaf, bell pepper flakes, cayenne pepper, celery seed, cilantro, cumin, fennel, garlic, ginger, Italian seasoning, mustard powder, poppy seed

Soups-Stews-bay leaf, bell pepper flakes, celery flakes, chives, cumin, gumbo file', nutmeg, parsley, sage, seafood seasoning, thyme, vegetable flakes

Vegetables-allspice, apple pie spice, basil, caraway seed, cayenne pepper, chives, dill, ginger, mace, nutmeg, paprika, parsley, turmeric

HERBS-SEASONINGS-SPICES
(Definition-origin-use)

ALLSPICE-dried pea-sized berry of the pimento plant...sharply delicate flavored spice that resembles a blend of cloves, cinnamon, and nutmeg. This spice comes whole and ground. Use: whole berries in hot teas, cider, apple juice, cranberry juice, and pickles...
Ground: cakes, cookies, pies, sauces, squash, and sweet potatoes or yams.

APPLE PIE SPICE-a commercial blend of cinnamon, nutmeg, and all spice. Use: apple pie and other apple dishes, sweet potatoes or yams, salad dressings for fresh fruit, French toast, coffee cakes, and cookies.

BASIL-a member of the mint family...the leaves of the herb have a mild aromatic odor...a warm, sweet, leafy and slightly licorice flavored herb...The leaves are processed whole and also ground...especially complementary to tomato dishes, fish, and sauces.

BAY LEAF-green leaf from the laurel tree...has a pungent, sweet herbaceous, floral, spice flavor...comes in whole leaf and should be removed from food before serving... use: soups, sauces, stews, Creole, fish, and marinates.

BELL PEPPER FLAKES-dehydrated chopped sweet red and green bell pepper...use: as you would fresh bell pepper...in soups, stews, sauces, and Creole.

CARAWAY SEED-plant grown in the Netherlands...It is a herb of the parsley family, having small spicy seeds...has a spicy smell and an aromatic taste of anise and dill...Use: to flavor meats, noodles, breads, potatoes, cabbage, and sauerkraut.

CAYENNE PEPPER-a very hot and pungent hot pepper made from the fruits or seed of several peppers from the Guinea pepper, chili pepper, and red pepper...use: sauces, fish, and vegetables.

CELERY-a vegetable that can be found in dry leaf form, seed, or combined with salt...dehydrated flakes and stalks are used in the celery flakes...use: soups, stews, sauces, and dips...The seeds are used in pickling, soups, sauces, dressings, and cole-slaw. Celery salt contains ground celery seeds and salt...use: appetizers, spreads, salads, soups, and meats.

CHIVES-sweet mild flavored herb of the onion family, similar to the green onion tops...use: dips, soups, stews, and vegetables.

CHILI POWDER-a blend of ground chili pepper, cumin, garlic, oregano and salt...use...chili, sauces, casseroles, and Cajun or Mexican dishes.

CILANTRO-also known as Chinese parsley...the leaf of the coriander plant...The cilantro and coriander seed have different flavors...use: salsa, soups, Mexican dishes such as burritos, tacos and enchiladas.

CINNAMON-spice that is the inner bark of several different tropical evergreen trees of the laurel family. The bark is stripped from the shoots on the tree and dried. As it dries, it curls into quills, known as cinnamon sticks. The sticks can be ground into a fine powder. Use: ground spice in cakes, cookies, puddings, pies, bread, and cooked fruit...stick can be used in hot tea, apple juice and cider, cranberry juice, and pickles.

CLOVES-spice extracted from the dried flower bulb of the clove tree, which are picked just before they open. Spice comes whole or ground. Use: ground cloves may be used in apple and pumpkin dishes, sweet potatoes and yams, beets, and baked beans...whole cloves can be used as studs for whole hams, mulled wine, hot spiced tea, hot apple cider, or hot apple juice and for pickled fruits such as pickled peaches.

CORIANDER-ground seed from the coriander plant...use: cakes, cookies, puddings, pastries, stuffing, chicken and fish dishes.

CUMIN-aromatic seed are cultivated from a dwarf plant native to Egypt and Syria...comes in seed form and also ground...Use: chili, Southwestern dishes, soups, sauces, and stews...cumin has a very distinct flavor, very strong and spicy.

CURRY POWDER-a special blend of ground bay leaves, black pepper, celery seeds, cloves, coriander, cumin, fenugreek, ginger, nutmeg, onion, red pepper and turmeric...use: Indian dishes, beef, chicken, lamb, shrimp, salads, and fruit.

DILL-herb that is a member of the parsley family...green in color, the plant has yellow flowers. It has an aromatic odor and a delicate caraway flavor...the weed itself can be ground and also the seed may be used. The dill weed is milder than the seed. Use: (dill weed) dips, salad dressings, stuffed eggs, salads, and fish...(the seed) dill pickles, cabbage, sauerkraut, spiced vinegar, potato salad.

FENNEL-tall herb that is a member of the parsley family...produces tiny yellow-brown seeds from the fruit of the plants...the leaves may also be used...has a sweet, hot, slightly licorice or anise-like flavor...use: fish, bread, salads, spreads, meat, sauces, and sweet pickles.

GARLIC-a bulbous herb of the lily family...is composed of smaller bulbs called cloves...very pungent and strong scented...when dried, it comes as minced, in a powder, and also mixed with salt and other herbs such as parsley...use: meat, fish, stews, soups, breads, sauces, marinades, and casseroles.

GINGER-an aromatic spice from a pungent root...comes in a ground form...use: cakes, cookies, puddings, Oriental dishes, sweet potatoes and yams, and salad dressings.

GUMBO FILE'-ground sassafras leaves...use: gumbos, jambalaya, Creole, and other Bayou dishes.

ITALIAN SEASONING-a blend of ground basil, marjoram, oregano, rosemary, sage, savory, and thyme. Use: Italian dishes such as sauces, casseroles, and marinades.

LEMON PEEL-very finely ground dried lemon peel...use: sweet potatoes and yams, muffins, cakes, cookies, carrots, and hot beverages.

MACE-spice from the dried covering around the nutmeg seed. The flavor is similar to nutmeg but with a fragrant, delicate difference. The spice is ground using the covering between the husk and the seed of the nutmeg. Use: vegetables, fruit pies, and cakes.

MARJORAM-gray-green perennial herb of the mint family...has a sweet mint flavor...comes as whole leaves or ground...use: chowder, dumplings, chicken, pork and eggs.

MUSTARD-a pungent, yellow in color, spice that comes from the seed of the mustard plant. This spice comes in a fine ground powder or small seed form. Use: dips, spreads, sauces, and pickles.

NUTMEG-the aromatic kernel of the fruit of the nutmeg tree...this spice comes ground or whole. Use: soups, chicken, sweet breads, fruits, puddings, and vegetables.

ONION-plant of the lily family with an edible bulb...has a pungent taste and odor. Dried onion seasonings come minced, chopped, flaked, in a powder, mixed with salt and as chopped green onion tops. Use: to flavor as you would with fresh onion...in meats, casseroles, soups, vegetables, dips, and spreads.

ORANGE PEEL-finely ground fresh orange peel...use: cakes, muffins, hot beverages, sweet potatoes and yams, squash, and carrots.

OREGANO- is a member of the mint family. It comes in leaf form and is light green in color. It has a strong aromatic odor. It has a slightly bitter taste. The leaf comes whole or ground. Use: stews, sauces, gravies, stuffing, vegetables, and salads.

PAPRIKA-a powder from the ground dry pod variety of the capsicum plant, which is a mild sweet red pepper, similar to the bell pepper...slightly aromatic and has a brilliant red color...use: as a garnish for salads and stuffed eggs and as a seasoning and topping.

PARSLEY-aromatic garden herb...the leaves, which are bright green, are used fresh or dried...adds color as well as flavor...use: soups, meats, stuffing, and dressings.

PEPPER-a pungent condiment obtained from an East Indian plant...the dried berries of this plant yield black pepper. The white pepper comes from the dried ripe seeds, without the coating. Pepper can come in different grinds, such as fine, medium, and course. It can also come whole, if you prefer to grind it yourself. Whole peppercorns can also be used for flavoring. This condiment can be purchased mixed with other herbs and seasonings, such as lemon pepper, parsley pepper, etc. Use: sauces, meats, soups, marinades, stews, and vegetables.

POPPY SEED-seed of the flower pod of the poppy plant...grown in Holland...the small black seed has a rich fragrance with a crunchy nut like flavor...the black seed has a slight slate blue color...use: dressings, breads, cookies, fruit salads, and sauces.

POULTRY SEASONING-a blend of ground allspice, coriander, marjoram, sage, thyme, and white pepper. Use: poultry, stuffing, and dressings.

PUMPKIN PIE SPICE-a blend of ground allspice, cloves, ginger, and nutmeg...use: pumpkin, sweet potatoes or yams, bread, and puddings.

ROSEMARY-a herb that comes from the leaf of a shrub like plant...looks like a short pine needle...has a sweet, fresh piney flavor...very aromatic...use: lamb, marinades, stuffing, seafood, and bread.

SAGE-a herb that comes from the leaves of a shrub or plant of the mint family...the gray-green leaves have a pleasant aromatic odor with a slightly bitter taste...comes whole or ground...use: poultry stuffing, chicken, sausage, pot roast, turkey, soups, chowders, and stews.

SEAFOOD SEASONING-a blend of ground celery seed, mustard, paprika, red pepper, salt, black pepper, ginger, allspice, bay leaf, cloves and cardamom...use: cooking shellfish, casseroles, chowders, soups, and stews.

TARRAGON-a European perennial plant related to the wormwood...the herb comes from the aromatic leaves of this plant...has a pungent, hot taste, resembling licorice...comes whole or ground...use: chicken, seafood, eggs, sauces, and dressings.

THYME-is a small shrub-like plant of the mint family. It has short brown leaves with a warm aromatic odor with a strong, distinctive, pungent flavor...can be found ground or whole...use: chicken, fish, lamb, vegetables, soups, and chowders.

TURMERIC-a ground powder obtained from a root of the ginger family...has a mild ginger-pepper flavor...use: eggs, pickling, relishes, seafood, sauces, and potatoes.

VANILLA POWDER-a commercial powder that is used instead of vanilla extract...use: cakes, cookies, fruits, desserts, and hot beverages.

VEGETABLE FLAKES-choice fresh vegetables that have been chopped and dried or dehydrated...contains dehydrated carrots, celery, tomatoes, onions, spinach, parsley, peppers, and potatoes...use: soups, stews, chowders, and casseroles.

EQUAL MEASURE

3 teaspoons = 1 tablespoon
24 teaspoons = ½ cup
48 teaspoons = 1 cup
8 tablespoons = ½ cup
12 tablespoons = ¾ cup
16 tablespoons = 1 cup

1 oz. liquid = 2 tablespoons
4 oz. liquid = ½ cup
8 oz. liquid = 1 cup
16 oz. liquid = 1 pint = 2 cups
32 oz. liquid = 1 quart = 4 cups

2 quarts = ½ gallon = 8 cups
4 quarts = 1 gallon = 16 cups

4 quarts = ½ peck
8 quarts = 1 peck
2 pecks = ½ bushel
4 pecks = 1 bushel

⅛ teaspoon garlic powder = 1 average garlic clove
1 teaspoon mustard powder = 1 tablespoon prepared mustard
1 teaspoon dried herbs = 1 tablespoon fresh herbs
1 tablespoon dried chopped onions = 1 small fresh onion

2 can = 20 oz. = 2 ½ cups
4 oz. cheese = 1 cup shredded cheese
1 (4 oz.) can sliced mushrooms = 8 oz. fresh mushrooms
1 (5 oz.) can chunk style chicken = ⅝ cup chopped fresh cooked chicken
1 (10 oz.) can chunk style chicken = 1 ¼ cup chopped fresh cooked chicken

1 cup regular brown sugar = 1 cup granulated brown sugar
1 teaspoon vanilla powder = 1 teaspoon vanilla extract
1 1/3 cup non-fat dry milk + 3 3/4 cups water = 1 quart liquid
3 tablespoons non-fat dry milk + 8 oz. water = 1 cup liquid

3 packages sugar substitute = 1/4 cup sugar
4 packages sugar substitute = 1/3 cup sugar
6 packages sugar substitute = 1/2 cup sugar
12 packages sugar substitute = 1 cup sugar

1/2 teaspoon butter flavored granules = 2 teaspoons butter
1 teaspoon butter flavored granules = 4 teaspoons butter
1 tablespoon butter flavored granules = 12 tablespoons butter
or 3/4 cup

16 oz. dry regular rice = 2 1/3 cups
16 oz. raisins = 3 1/2 cups
1 stick margarine or butter = 1/2 cup
1/2 stick margarine or butter = 1/4 cup
2 sticks margarine or butter = 1 cup

30 saltine crackers (crushed) = 1 cup cracker crumbs
32 vanilla wafers (crushed) = 1 cup vanilla wafer crumbs
14 graham cracker squares (crushed) = 1 cup graham cracker crumbs
4 slices dry bread (crumbed) = 1 cup dry bread crumbs

1 medium green pepper = 1 cup chopped green pepper
1 small potato = 1 cup cubed potato
3 medium oranges = 1 cup orange juice
8 small green onions = 1 cup sliced green onions
1 medium lemon = 2 to 3 tablespoons lemon juice
1 medium lemon = 2 to 3 teaspoons grated lemon peel
1 small apple = 1 cup chopped apple
1 lb. cabbage = 4 cups shredded cabbage
2 medium carrots = 1 cup grated carrots
3 medium carrots = 1 cup sliced carrots
2 stalks celery = 1 cup sliced celery

GRAB A BAG

8 oz. dry uncooked macaroni = 2 cups uncooked macaroni = 4 cups cooked macaroni

8 oz. uncooked spaghetti noodles = 2 cups uncooked noodles = 4 cups cooked noodles

8 oz. uncooked egg noodles = 4 cups uncooked noodles = 4 cups cooked noodles

1 cup uncooked regular rice = 3 to 4 cups cooked rice

1 cup uncooked quick cooking or minute rice = 1 1/3 cup cooked rice

1 1/3 cup instant potato flakes = 2 cups prepared potatoes = 1 lb. fresh potatoes

1 cup cleaned shrimp = 3/4 lb. raw shrimp in the shell = 7 oz. package frozen peeled shrimp = 1 (5 oz.) can of shrimp

There are four full sized patterns for "Make your own recipe cards", on the following pages. Trace selected motif and transfer to an index card. Paint or color motif, cut, and paste to a second 3" x 5" index card, which has been folded, as indicated in the drawings on the next two pages. Write the recipe for completing on the inside of the card and attach to your bag.

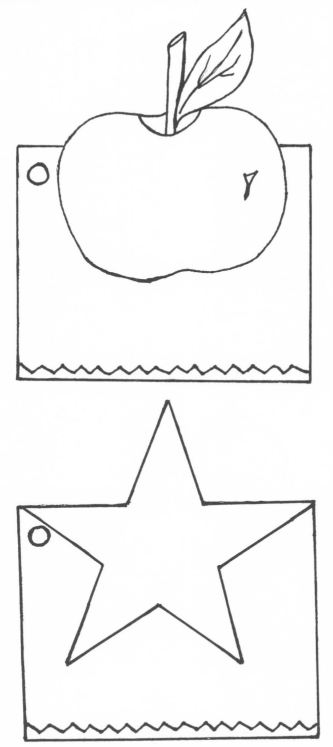

– INDEX –

APPETIZERS

BEVERAGES

BREADS AND MUF-FINS

ET CETERA

GRAB A BAG

MAIN DISH

SIDE DISH

SOUPS

SWEETS